FLORIDA, EH?

A **Canadian Guide** to the **Sunshine State**

BY ISOBEL WARREN AND MILAN CHVOSTEK

The undiscovered, unsung, unspoiled Florida

CEDAR CAVE BOOKS
Newmarket, ON
September, 2002

905-895-9296; 1-866-895-9296; **info@florida-eh.com**
For updates and more info visit **www.florida-eh.com**

Florida, Eh? A Canadian Guide to the Sunshine State
By Isobel Warren and Milan Chvostek
Design by Sandra Peic
Printed in Canada by Cober Printing Ltd., Kitchener, ON.

ISBN: 0-920403-12-3

Cedar Cave Books, Box 180, Newmarket, ON L3Y 4X1
1-866-895-9296 ✪ info@florida-eh.com ✪ www.florida-eh.com

Every effort has been made to ensure the accuracy of information published in this book. The authors and the publisher assume no liability, direct or indirect, to any person or party for any loss or damage in regard to errors or omis-
sions of any kind.

National Library of Canada Cataloguing in Publication

Warren, Isobel, Florida, eh? : a Canadian guide to the sunshine state /
by Isobel Warren and Milan Chvostek.

Includes index.

ISBN 0-920403-12-3

1. Florida--Guidebooks. I. Chvostek, Milan II. Title.

F309.3.W37 2002   917.5904'64   C2002-902933-3

CONTENTS

Florida – undiscovered, unsung, unspoiled.

The undiscovered, unsung, unspoiled Florida . . .
people and places, water and wilderness,
history and culture, food and lodging . . .
unique views of the Florida that's hidden,
forgotten and waiting to be revealed.

Step by step, mile by mile

This & That, Here & There

Florida, Eh? Take a second look . . .

Don't dismiss Florida. Far from the theme parks and body-crush beaches, lifestyles away from shuffleboard and bingo, another Florida is waiting to be discovered – untrammeled wilderness and eco-adventures, swashbuckling history and rich culture, stunning seascapes and isolated beaches, creative cuisine and outstanding lodgings, remarkable people and quirky attractions – beyond the hype, around the corner, off the beaten track.

As a prime winter destination, Florida knows a thing or three about hospitality. And as the closest warm winter destination for Eastern Canada, easily accessible by car, air and train, it's been a Canadian favourite for decades.

But Florida, Eh? set out to discover a different Florida. And even we were astounded by the state's wealth of unsung, unusual and unique attractions that Canadians rarely hear about.

This book reflects our personal journey, our tastes and prejudices. We ferreted out historic towns and regions, little-known features, unique lodgings and eateries. They range from ultra-luxurious to budget, from ultra-chic to rustic. All are worthy of note.

So don't dismiss Florida. Leaf through *Florida, Eh?* to find the Sunshine State's hidden treasures. And please visit our website – www.florida-eh.com – to share your experiences and collect more good leads.

Bon voyage.

Isobel Warren and Milan Chvostek
Newmarket, Canada
September, 2002

If you pause to explore Florida's northeastern corner – and you really should – you may never venture further south. Southern hospitality, rich history, temperate weather, good beaches, fine food and interesting lodgings all contribute to your entrapment.

In days of yore …

Since Europeans first landed in Florida nearly five centuries ago, (decades before the Pilgrims waded ashore at Plymouth Rock), St. Augustine, and equally historic Fernandina Beach on Amelia Island, have changed hands more often than the Stanley Cup.

Old St. Augustine Village is a fine starting point to explore the area's history.

Spanish adventurer Don Juan Ponce de Leon claimed the land for Spain in 1513, naming it La Florida – the Land of Flowers. Poor Don Juan thought he had discovered the Fountain of Youth but the spring he found, still promoted in St. Augustine, failed to stop the aging process.

Half a century later the French arrived, establishing a fort to harass Spanish treasure fleets. That annoyed the Spanish so they sent an army that wiped out the French garrison – with a little help from a passing hurricane – and established St. Augustine.

Next came the Brits, amusing themselves with frequent assaults on the Spaniards. Finally, in 1763, Spain ceded Florida to England, just in time for the American Revolution. In 1783, the state went back to Spain who finally sold it to the United States in 1821 for $5 million.

Those centuries of wall-to-wall wars caused untold hardship, devastation and death, but flag makers prospered. Eight flags, including the stars and stripes, have flown over Amelia Island, some of them for just a day or two.

St. Augustine

St. Augustine's Spanish heritage is still in evidence. **Castillo de San Marcos**, the Spanish fort built to withstand the British, still guards the harbour. Built of coquina, a soft limestone of broken shells, its ability to absorb cannon balls rather than crumble helped the fort withstand two major attacks in the 1700s. These days, it's still regularly invaded -- by fleets of luxury yachts and hordes of tourists.

In modern times ...

St. Augustine retained its sleepy image until the 1880s when railway tycoon **Henry Flagler**, who built a rail line from Jacksonville to Key West, earmarked the town as a luxury resort, building fine hotels, churches, a railway station and public areas. His magnificent Ponce de Leon Hotel, now **Flagler College**, began life as a posh resort for wealthy northerners. His churches too are interesting – he built churches of various denominations including the Flagler Memorial Presbyterian where he rests in the adjoining mausoleum.

Arches and turrets, red tile roofs and stained glass accent the grand style of century-old Flagler College.

The town boasts many 'firsts' and 'oldests'. Downtown St. George Street, open only to pedestrians, is home to the oldest house in America, the oldest wooden schoolhouse and the oldest store.

Lightner Museum ✪75 King St., St. Augustine 32085 ✪ 904-824-2874
✪ www.LightnerMuseum.org

The Lightner Museum, built as an hotel in 1888, displays a fascinating collection of 'stuff' assembled by Otto C. Lightner, a publisher and advocate of hobbies and collecting. He practiced what he preached – the museum is a breath-taking treasure trove of cut glass, matchbook covers, buttons, rare furniture, clocks, statuary, a mummy and an 1873 piano –

furniture, ceramics, textiles, glass, scientific and natural history artifacts plus a 6,000-volume research library.

And music boxes – from dainty to full piano size. Daily demonstrations of these rare and beautiful mechanical musical instruments must not be missed. The German Orchestrion, built in 1874, is a complete orchestra in one case with a 45-note piano, three ranks of pipes, a glockenspiel, cymbals, snare drum and bass drum. And all it needs is a turn of the crank. The Violano-Virtuoso incorporates both a piano and a violin. Various music boxes that work from huge perforated steel disks, a Swiss cylinder music box from 1890, a foot-pumped player organ and a hand-cranked 20-note reed organ are other treasures.

The Lightner contains many reminders of the grand style of the 1800s. This was, after all, the Alcazar, one of Flagler's flagship hotels. In its day, its 120-foot indoor pool (now shops and dining) was the world's largest. What's more, it was fed by unfiltered sulphur water from an artesian well -- now covered by a parking lot, for heaven sake! Open 9-5 daily.

Old St. Augustine Village, (operated by the Museum of Arts and Sciences of Daytona Beach) ✪ *246 St. George St., St. Augustine, 32084* ✪ *904-823-9722* ✪ *www.old-staug-village.com*

Old St. Augustine Village is a recent addition to the historic grid of this lovely old town and very welcome too, for its ten buildings seem to encapsulate the real life of the town from the 1700s to the early 1900s.

The oldest building is a cute little pink house dating from 1790, once

the home of Prince Napoleon Achille Murat, Napoleon's nephew, who had a brief fling with St. Augustine in 1824 before heading north to marry George Washington's grand-niece. Two later houses, the 1839 Dow House and the 1840 Canova House exhibit very different styles of décor and furnishings. The 1899 Star General Store serves as a wel-

Napoleon's nephew lived here. Collection of historic buildings makes for absorbing tour.

come centre. As well, there's a 1904 carpenter's house and several pri-vate homes of varying vintages.

The houses and encircling wall surround charming courtyards with trees and gardens, fountains and benches that invite quiet contemplation of St. Augustine's turbulent past and pleasant present. Guided tours are offered each hour daily or you can tour on your own, informed by a succinct brochure available from the visitor centre. Admission: $7 adults, $6 seniors, $5 children.

Beyond the waterway ...

Cross the **Bridge of Lions**, (be patient – it may be undergoing restoration) and you're headed toward 50 miles of white sand -- **St. Augustine Beach, Ponte Vedra Beach, Anastasia Island** and **Jacksonville Beach**.

But first, pay a visit to two establishments that have been championing the cause of wildlife for decades – **the Alligator Farm** and **Marineland**.

Alligator Farm ✪ 999 Anastasia Blvd., St. Augustine ✪ 904-824-3337 ✪
www.alligatorfarm.com

Meet the folks – from a safe distance – at Alligator Farm, home to all 23 species of the world's crocodilians.

The Alligator Farm harbours much more than prehistoric reptiles. Besides all 23 species of the world's crocodilians, both alligators and crocodiles, you'll see birds such as snowy egrets, herons and parrots, kookeburra and possum, deer, spider monkeys, tortoises and various other reptiles and mammals. Board walks elevate you safely over pools of sunbathing alligators, all looking deceptively docile. Daily shows exhibiting alligators, reptiles and inhabitants of the rainforest may indicate otherwise. You'll also meet **Gomek**, a giant New Guinea crocodile – all 17 feet and 2,000 pounds of him, laid out by an expert taxidermist. Especially remarkable are rare albino alligators which, in Cajun folklore, are supposed to bring luck to those who see them. So don't miss that pool near the main entrance.

Marineland Oceanarium ✪ 9600 Ocean Shore Blvd., St. Augustine ✪ 1-888-279-9194 ✪ www.marineland.net Open 9:30 - 4:30 daily except Tuesday. Adults $14; kids $9.

Marineland of Florida, the world's first Oceanarium, is getting a new lease on life. Established in 1938, Marineland – home to 11 dolphins, two of them born in 2002, plus flamingos, sea lions, black-footed penguins, sea turtles and hundreds of fish – is poised to emerge as a centre for research, especially in the realm of dolphin therapy for kids with special needs. The current project, however, is restoration of the site, which had fallen upon hard times before new owner Jim Jacoby rescued it and embarked on a program of renovation and redevelopment. He's creating a 42-acre Marineland town, right across the street, revitalizing an old marina and adding a small resort, garden apartments, beach club and town centre. A popular Marineland feature is the **Dolphin Encounter**, a 40-minute program that lets visitors (50 inches or taller) interact with dolphins in the water. It begins with a session with a dolphin trainer, then you suit up and hop into the pool, under the trainer's supervision. $120, reservations required. **Dolphin Touch and Feed**: $19.95.

And so to bed and breakfast ...

St. Augustine's gracious old homes lend themselves to bed and breakfast inns. Genuinely hospitable hosts, divine breakfasts, unique décor and furniture, and lovingly preserved old homes are their hallmarks.

Kenwood Inn ✪ ($$) ✪ 38 Marine St., St. Augustine 32084 ✪ 904-824-2116 www.oldcity.com/kenwood

At the Kenwood Inn in St. Augustine, we found a Canadian connection – host Mark Constant traces his family tree back to French Canada. He and his wife, Kerrianne, are a well-travelled couple whose comfortable home, built in 1865, features 14 guest rooms and a wraparound upper verandah fitted with comfy rockers. Meticulously maintained, it's furnished with interesting antiques in spacious and well appointed non-smoking rooms. There's a small swimming pool and a picturesque koi pond in the courtyard.

Getting acquainted is easy, thanks to an evening wine hour and a pre-dinner nip of sherry. Coffee, tea and habit-forming chocolate chip cookies are on hand throughout the day.

Breakfast turns decadent thanks to Kerrianne's cranberry scones, orange mandarin cake and banana bread, served with a fruit plate and yogurt. But you can work it all off by borrowing wheels from the complimentary bike fleet, and touring the historic district.

Victorian House ✪ *($$)* ✪ *11 Cadiz, St. Augustine 32084* ✪ *904-824-4215* ✪ *1- 877-576-7742* ✪ *www.victorianhouseinn.com*

The Victorian House, just steps away from the Kenwood, is hosted by Ken and Marcia Cerotzke who call themselves 'corporate drop-outs' – escapees from the business bustle of Chicago to the historic charm of St. Augustine. Ken, president of the **Historic Inns Association**, is a gold-mine of information about his adopted city, its festivals and amenities.

Their house, built in 1897, was carefully restored in 1993. Eight spacious rooms are named for the original owner's children, in-laws and friends. Country antiques decorate Juli's room, while Daisy prefers ruffles and lace and Hanna favours teddy bears and hearts. Jennifer's room has a lovely 1870 spool canopy bed while Pauline's boasts a private entrance and porch. We enjoyed Laura's suite (one of four suites in the carriage house) which, with private entrance, enclosed sunporch and neat kitchenette, plus a king-size bed and two singles, is an ideal family roost. (Children are welcomed in the carriage house.) The innkeepers aren't kidding about their non-smoking policy. They levy a $100 surcharge if they find any evidence of smoking in a room.

Breakfast is memorable -- home made granola, tasty quiche or other hot dish and Marsha's sweet cakes. Coffee is ready an hour beforehand.

Victorian House offers readers of Florida, Eh? a 10 per cent discount if you show or mention this book.

Old City House Inn and Restaurant ✪ *($$-$$$)* ✪ *115 Cordova St., St. Augustine, 32084* ✪ *904-826-0113 (Inn), 904-826-0184 (Restaurant)* ✪ *www.oldcityhouse.com*

Seven antique-furnished rooms plus an upscale restaurant opened in 2001 comprise this 1873 house in the heart of historic downtown. Well-travelled hosts James and Ilse Philcox and their staff speak English,

Spanish and Afrikaans and touches of English and African décor recall their origins. **Old City House** was named best upscale restaurant in St. Augustine in 2002. Many an international influence pervades the dinner menu – Thai curry or Mahi Bermuda. Or even drunken pig – loin pork chops in a beer and ginger marinade, served on pickled red cabbage with apple pecan chutney. Entrée prices are typically under $20; reservations are recommended. A full cooked breakfast is served and on weekends James and Ilse host a cheese and wine evening social. Bicycles are available to guests.

St. Francis Inn ✺ *($$-$$$)* ✺ *279 St. George St., St. Augustine 32084* ✺ *1-800-824-6062* ✺ *904-824-6068* ✺ *www.stfrancisinn.com*

Just around the corner from the oldest house, you'll find the oldest inn – **St. Francis Inn**, built in 1791 in a style decreed by the King of Spain 'to serve as a defense against those who might attempt to occupy the town.' Thus the house abuts the street, shielding the entrance and courtyard. These days, however, the King of Spain would be startled to find a swimming pool, luxurious private baths, air conditioning, queen or king-sized beds and cable TV. Several rooms have fireplaces, kitchenettes and whirlpool tubs. Complimentary bicycles and admission to the St. Augustine Lighthouse are offered to guests. The

Romantic carriage rides clip-clop through ancient streets – perfect for sightseeing.

buffet breakfast menu is eclectic, ranging from ham and cheese pie to piggy pudding, southern grits to tomato quiche, mandarin muffins to strawberry soup. Coffee, tea and pastries are available 'round the clock and complimentary evening socials help break the ice.

St. Francis Inn offers Canadians who mention Florida, Eh? at reservation time a 15% discount (Sun–Thurs during non-holiday periods).

Historic Inns of St. Augustine, representing some 25 of the city's most appealing establishments, has an 'inn-on-call' service, that helps to find you a vacancy if the inn or B&B that you call is full. The same service is on line – www.staugustineinns.com

The group also co-ordinates various promotions. June is designated **Senior Sweethearts Month** when the innkeepers create a package especially for mature lovers, who are perhaps celebrating an anniversary, renewing their wedding vows or simply falling in love again. Besides special rates, an add-on package includes a private horse-drawn carriage ride, trolley tours and tickets to various museums. Details are on the website.

Casa Monica Hotel ✪
($$$) ✪ *95 Cordova St.,*
St. Augustine 32084 ✪
1-800-648-1888 ✪
www.casamonica.com

New lease on life finds Hotel Casa Monica, opened in 1888, restored to its earlier splendour with many extra perks.

One of St. Augustine's handsomest and most historic hotels – promoted as the oldest hotel in the oldest city in America – the **Casa Monica** recently enjoyed a $17 million renovation. It's a romantic sight – a Moorish revival castle with lavish towers, arches, and a red tile roof. Its 138 rooms include 14 signature suites, most of them two and three stories. The most popular, the Ponce de Leon suite, has a third-story Jacuzzi room overlooking the town and Montanza Bay. The 95 Cordova restaurant, the Cobalt Lounge and the Deli Market and Coffee Shop offer dining from formal to casual. The hotel's fleet of classic antique cars, including a 1929 Model A Ford convertible, a 1930 Ford Model A hardtop and a 1955 Chrysler Imperial, is available for guided tours and weddings.

The Casa Monica is just across the street from the equally romantic looking Alcazar, now the **Lightner Museum** and kitty-corner from the Ponce de Leon Hotel, now **Flagler College**. Opened in 1888 and sold soon afterward to the intrepid Henry Flagler, the hotel succumbed to the Depression in 1932 and stood empty for 30 years. The St. John County Commission bought it in 1962 for $250,000 and converted it to a court-house. In 1999, it was reborn as the Casa Monica.

Pirate Haus Inn and Hostelodge ✪ *($)* ✪ *32 Treasury St., St. Augustine 32084* ✪ *904-808-1999* ✪ *www.PirateHaus.com*

Pirate Haus Inn and Hostelodge, a member of **Hostelling International**, woos bargain-hunters of all ages with affordable prices, private or dorm rooms, and all-you-can-eat breakfasts – all the fixin's are supplied in the shared guest kitchen where you can also prepare other meals. This merry place, with its colourful air-conditioned rooms and pirate theme, offers free tea and coffee all day, free local calls, free stays for kids 12 and under ('bunkaneers' receive free pirate hats). The com-mon room is stocked with a guitar, games, books and a six-foot pirate. Besides standard hostel dorms, there are private rooms with deep old-fashioned bathtubs (anyone for in-house snorkeling?), a rooftop patio, barbeque and Internet access. Guests are walking distance from most of St. Augustine's prime attractions and Pirate Haus plies them with dozens of discount tickets for carriage and boat rides, ghost walks, museums, restaurants and shopping.

Another unusual feature is the inn's 'Guest Who's Coming to Dinner' program which connects guests with local families – a special boon for foreign travellers keen to experience American life.

Eats and drinks . . .

As you can imagine, St. Augustine offers a vast range of dining choices, from ultra-luxurious to junk. We sought out the places that seemed fun and affordable but two people can only eat so much . . . so do sample some of the ones we've missed and tell us about them.

Gypsy Cab Company Bar & Grill ✪ *($$)* ✪ *828 Anastasia Blvd.* ✪ *904- 824-8244* ✪ *www.gypsycab.com*

Tasty food in a fun and funky atmosphere make this a jolly place for lunch, dinner or an evening of comedy. Watch for a violet-painted building that looks for all the world like a taxi dispatch office with attitude. Which is precisely what it is, combining a restaurant, open for dinner only, a bar and grill open for lunch and evening entertainment and a comedy club. Inside, it sports a black ceiling, and a hilarious wall mural depicting a collection of dippy mutts, old cars, alligators and pelicans. The Gypsy Bar and Grill, serves light bar fare with live music. Lunch is served weekdays from 11 to 4. Next door, the **Comedy Club** offers a double-act show of stand-up laughs from Thursday to Saturday.

Florida Cracker Café ✪ ($) ✪ 81 St. George St. ✪ 904-829-0397

Florida crackers were early farmers and cowboys, named for the crack of their whips as they herded cattle. Their menu probably didn't run to Philly Cheese Steak Sandwiches or Fried Mozzarella Cheese Sticks but you can imagine them chowing down on all kinds of seafood, cornbread, fritters or crab cakes. You'll find all those and more at the **Florida Cracker Café** on pedestrian-only St. George Street. There's dining inside at the bar or at tables and outside at picnic tables under aromatic jasmine trees. Casual, fun and affordable, it's at the centre of all the action.

Harry's Seafood Bar and Grille ✪ ($-$$) ✪ 46 Avenida Menendez ✪ 904-824-7765 ✪ www.HookedonHarrys.com

Harry's Seafood Bar and Grille is part of a small chain (others in Jacksonville Beach and Jacksonville, Ocala, Lakeland and Gainesville.) Open for lunch and dinner, it boasts a hefty menu that's understandably heavy on seafood but offers up chicken, steaks and pasta as well. There's definitely a Cajun flavour to this menu – Jambalaya, Crawfish or Shrimp Etoufee, Louisiana Gumbo and blackened this and that. Prices are moderate, the mood is upbeat, kids are welcome.

Hip Hypolita

Several appealing little eateries keep company on tiny Hypolita Street, which extends three blocks or so from the waterfront to Cordova.

The Tea Room, 15 Hypolita St. ✪ 904-808-8395

The Tea Room serves a dozen or more varieties of tea along with fresh salads, from $3.95 to $6.50, sandwiches from $4.75 to $5.45 and afternoon tea with sandwiches and scones at $7.50. French, Dutch, German and English are spoken. Open for lunch and afternoon tea, Wed to Sun.

Schmagel's Bagels and Deli, 69 Hypolita St. ☺ *904-824-4444*

A cheerful breakfast spot is **Schmagel's** – 10 varieties of fresh-baked bagels with as many spreads, (at $2 for plain cream cheese to $5.50 for lox and cream cheese) or with sausage, egg and cheese (at $3.50). Lunch offers sandwiches and salads, again modestly priced. Concrete benches at the courtyard tables are comfortably covered with braided rugs. Open daily from 7 a.m. (8 on Sundays).

Walking with history's ghosts

St. Augustine has become a hot spot for cold chills. With the Spaniards massacring the natives, then demolishing an entire French army and tossing it into the bay, and with the usual roster of murders, fires and plagues such as yellow fever, it seemed a lot of folks died untimely and violent deaths. And it seems they've all come back to search for their former lives, limbs and loved ones. Ghosts are big business in St. Augustine and ghostly tours of one kind and another abound, some of them short on ghosts but long on laughs. Our ghostly host, an actor posing as a gravedigger of yore, led us through darkened streets, pointing out ghosts on balconies and at windows, then through a pitch-black graveyard for more gory tales. Next we boarded a trolley train, to visit the Old City Jail where a ghostly 'inmate' introduced us to a real working gallows. Half a dozen or more companies offer ghost walks. You can book them at your hotel or B&B, or at kiosks throughout the town.

World Golf Village and World Golf Hall of Fame ☺ *I-95 at exit 95A, St. Augustine 32092* ☺ *1-800-948-4643* ☺ *www.wgv.com* ☺ *Guided tours 3 times daily. Vacation packages and Golf Academy. ($$$$).*

This region has a long association with golf. In fact, back in the 1880s, the St. Augustine Golf Club operated a golf course on the grounds of the old fort. The World Golf Village complex includes the World Golf Hall of Fame, a golf academy offering private lessons and multi-day golf schools; a retail centre and two championship courses, including the King & Bear, the first-ever golf course design collaboration between legends Jack Nicklaus and Arnold Palmer. A golf-themed restaurant is the Murray Bros. **Caddyshack**, owned and operated by actor-comedian Bill Murray and his five brothers, and named for their Caddyshack movie. It's the first in a string that may include locations in Canada.

Greeting visitors entering the **World Golf Hall of Fame** is a replica of the golf club that astronaut Alan Shepard used in 1971 when he stepped onto the moon from Apollo 14 and whacked an innocent golf ball some 1,500 yards – one-handed, if you please. Other historic artifacts and some high-tech exhibits recall the history and most memorable moments of this ancient sport, right from its beginnings in Scotland. You can even try out a wooden club and 'guttie' – the gutta percha ball used in the 1800s. There are histories of many outstanding golfers, along with photos, video clips and personal mementoes. The complex includes several major hotels, a six-story IMAX theatre, Sam Snead's Tavern and shops.

St. Augustine Events

Nights of Lights – Historic re-enactments, Christmas tours of historic inns and homes – December

Regatta of Lights – Matanzas Bay parade of lighted vessels – December

Blessing of the Fleet – Noon, Palm Sunday. All done up in their best bunting, both pleasure and commercial craft form a procession to the city marina to receive the blessing of the Bishop of the Diocese of St. Augustine

Easter Parade – Marching bands, floats and St. Augustine's carriage horses modelling Easter bonnets.

Fernandina and Amelia Island

Amelia Island, a barrier island at Florida's northeast corner, but tucked under Georgia's southeast wing, is an upscale enclave where the wealthy and the wannabees are pampered with every amenity.

But there's more here than hedonism. This island manages to pack a passel of attractions and amenities into its 11,600 acres – history, charm, beautiful beaches, lovely B&Bs, and good seafood.

In **Fernandina Beach**, an entire 50-block downtown area is listed in the National Registry of Historic Places.

Amelia Island's post-European history is long and chequered. The French landed in 1562, swiftly displaced in 1565 by the Spanish who held on, more or less, for two centuries. The English arrived and conquered in 1763 but ceded the island, then known as Egmont, back to Spain in 1783. When Jefferson's Embargo Act of 1807 closed U.S. ports to foreign shipping, Fernandina became a bustling headquarters for smugglers and pirates. The Spaniards were briefly ousted in 1812 by the 'Patriots of Amelia Island', assisted secretly by the U.S., and again in 1817 by a group, flying the Green Cross of Florida. They were joined by the pirate Luis Aury who flew the Mexican Rebel Flag until U.S. troops routed him later that year. The Spanish handed over the island to the U.S. in 1821 and all was quiet until Civil War Confederates briefly took possession in 1861. The feds grabbed it back in 1862 and it has managed to fly the stars and stripes ever since.

The last quarter of the 19th century was Fernandina's heyday – gun-running in support of the Spanish American war coupled with tourism as visitors arrived by steamer, direct from New York City. Shrimping was big business in the early 1900s but tourism ultimately won the day.

It's quieter today – no gun-running, precious little overt piracy. The indigo plantations that briefly satisfied Europe's hunger for blue dye before the American Revolution are no more.

Fort Clinch State Park, North end of Amelia Island ❂ 904-277-7274 ❂ Open 8 to sundown. Fort open 9 to 5. Admission charged.

Fort Clinch, begun in 1847 but rendered obsolete by improved killing machines, comes alive the first weekend of each month when volunteers and park rangers re-enact life in 1864. Demonstrations of cooking and food, laundry and crafts reflect the period when the area was occupied by Union troops.

Amelia Island Museum of History ❂233 South Third St., Fernandina Beach, Fla. 32034 ❂ 904-261-7378 ❂ www.ameliaislandmuseumofhistory.org ❂ Mon-Fri, 10-5, Sat 10-4. Admission charged.

The Amelia Island Museum of History in Fernandina helps to keep the area's history vibrantly alive. It offers guided tours of the town, with its fabulous old mansions, dripping with gingerbread, stained glass and charm. There are ghost tours and a Cemetery Crawl, visiting one of the town's oldest cemeteries. (Tours: $8 for historic district, $15 for longer itineraries, advance reservations required.) The Museum also hosts a six-week Elderhostel program each winter.

The Museum is imprisoned in the old Nassau County Jail. With just four paid staff and a treasury of volunteers – in the first quarter of last year,

120 of them donated 1,265 hours – it can set many a bigger museum on its ear. Creative docents in period costume impersonate historic characters or, dressed as pirates, recount rattling true tales of piracy.

Kayak Amelia ✪ *1-888-30-KAYAK* ✪ *904-321-0697* ✪
(www.kayakamelia.com) offers guided kayak/nature tours.

Jody and Ray Hetchka start off with a short lesson before exploring the salt marshes of the Talbot State Park and Timucuan Ecological and Historical Preserve, inhabited by the native people over 5000 years ago. Guests may find themselves eye to eye with egrets, herons and perhaps a dolphin, while osprey and bald eagles glide overhead.

Amelia Island B&Bs

Although Amelia Island bed and breakfast hosts pride themselves on their hospitality, very few of them bother to spend the extra pennies for toll-free numbers accessible from Canada.

Addison House ✪ *($$)* ✪ *614 Ash St., Amelia Island* ✪ *904-277-1604* ✪
www.addison-housebb.com

Amelia's rebels and pirates have given way to quieter lifestyle, with fine B&Bs such as Addison House.

John and Donna Gibson arrived in Fernandina Beach in 1996. Their handsome property encompasses 14 rooms, spread through the main 1876 house plus a garden house and cottage. Rooms feature four-poster beds, antique furniture and sculptural accents that John creates between his duties as innkeeper, gardener and guests' helper. Fountains punctuate the pleasant garden. Breakfast is included and

Luxury furnishings, gourmet breakfasts and attentive hosts make the Ash Street Inn a welcome addition.

cookies and lemonade are afternoon refreshments.

Ash Street Inn ✪ *($$$)* ✪
102 South Seventh Street,
Amelia Island 32034 ✪
904 277-4941 ✪
www.ashstinn.com

Newly minted innkeepers Rob Tate and Chris Ludlam recently bought, renovated and renamed this 10-room inn, introducing subtle touches of luxury. The property comprises an 1880 guest house and a 1904 mansion. Each room includes king or queen size beds, private baths, quality soaps and robes, Jacuzzi or claw-foot tubs and intimate verandahs. The lavish breakfast could run to apple-caramel French toast or blueberry strata and vegetarians are catered to. Children under 12 and smoking are graciously refused as are large dogs. But complimentary bikes, beach towels and beach chairs are all provided.

A 15 per cent discount is offered to any reader who mentions 'Florida, Eh?' at reservation time at the Ash Street Inn.

Bailey House Victorian B&B ✪ *($$$)* ✪ *28 S. 7th Street, Fernandina Beach 32034* ✪
904-261-5390 ✪
www.bailey-house.com

Magnificent stained glass, richly carved wood and rare Victoriana adorn this 10-room Queen Anne mansion. From the formal parlour where classical music plays up the elaborate staircase to

Fernandina's B&Bs, including Bailey House, carefully preserve gracious details of historic settings.

the guest rooms with their fine antique furnishings, it's a handsome sight. Ten fireplaces, a deep wrap-around verandah with rocking chairs and of course, a full home-made breakfast that may include orange French toast or rosevine bake along with homemade granola are features. A private carriage house hideaway has its own verandah and separate entrance. Guests are limited to non-smokers, with no pets and no youngsters under eight.

Elizabeth Pointe Lodge ✪ *($$$)* ✪ *98 S. Fletcher Ave., Amelia Island 32034* ✪ *904 277-4851* ✪ *www.elizabethpointelodge.com*

Learn the fine art of B&B hosting or simply sit back and be pampered at Elizabeth Pointe Lodge in Fernandina Beach.

If you've ever considered opening a B&B, you've come to the right place. Susan and David Caples offer courses in acquiring and running a B&B, based on their many years of innkeeping in Fernandina Beach. Meanwhile, they practice what they preach in their 25-room lodge, where former Montrealer Barbara Bailey presides over the front desk. Perched high above the ocean, the lodge wins friends for its pleasant rooms, lavish buffet breakfast and a menu of soups, sandwiches and salads 'round the clock. Gathered in the lounge, with a cosy fire on cool days, a ravishing view of the beach and ocean from the deck outside, guests can enjoy a pre-dinner social hour with complimentary wine and hors d'oeuvres.

1857 Florida House Inn & Restaurant ✪ *($-$$$)* ✪ *Box 688, 20 and 22 South 3rd St., Amelia Island* ✪ *904 261-3300* ✪ *www.floridahouseinn.com*

The oldest continuously operating inn in Florida, this 15-room establishment, bedecked with Amelia Island's eight flags, is enhanced by a fully licensed pub, serving cocktails, wine and many varieties of beer. The inn offers three meals daily; breakfast is included in the room rate. Lunches and dinners (Tuesday to Saturday) and Sunday brunch ($) feature southern cooking, served boarding house style. Evening wine and cheese, beach towels and chairs, all-day coffee and iced tea, high speed Internet access are all offered and even kids and pets are tolerated.

Amelia Island Plantation ✪ *($$$-$$$$)* ✪ *Amelia Island* ✪ *1-800 874-6878* ✪ *904 261-6161* ✪ *www.aipfl.com*

Amelia Island Plantation occupies some 1,350 acres of the island, a luxurious haven that includes 670 rooms and villas, three 18-hole golf courses, 23 tennis courts, eight eateries. Its recently added spa, with 25 treatment rooms and a massage for every muscle, features a meditation garden and exotic seaweed, mud and aromatherapy. The Atlantic's snowy beaches plus 23 on-site swimming pools, seven miles of nature trails, horseback riding, fishing and sailing provide outdoor fun. Supervised programs for tads, teens and young adults include a day camp for ages three to ten, a raft of fun for the 11-19 crowd with culinary and beauty classes, kayaking, evening parties, bonfires and sports. In short, there's something for everyone – or at least for everyone who's prepared for rates that start at CDN$250 a day.

Amelia Island Events

Isle of Eight Flags Shrimp Festival ✪ *Amelia Island* ✪ *866-4-AMELIA* ✪ *904-261-3248* ✪ *www.shrimpfestival.com – First weekend of May.*

Shrimps and pirates – two of Amelia Island's historic realities– are stars of this lively festival in **Fernandina Beach**. A juried arts and crafts show attracts some 300 artisans and 100 antique dealers. But shrimp reigns or do we mean rains? About three dozen local non-profit groups – churches, clubs, firefighters, police, even the high school band and cheerleaders – set up booths to sell every conceivable style of shrimp, prepared from their secret recipes. Shrimp fans can graze from booth to booth, pausing to witness each evening's pirate invasion – the rambunctious **Fernandina Pirates Club**, replete with shrimp boats and pirate gear, plus a fireworks display. Sunday brings a Blessing of the Fleet and Best Decorated Shrimp Boat Contest.

Amelia Island Chamber Music Festival ☎ *904-277-1779* ☻ *www.ameliaislandchambermusic.org*

Palace Saloon once hosted pirates and renegades, more recently 'Beer and G-Strings' chamber music concert.

With its debut in June, 2002, this two-week festival presented an ambitious program of chamber music, featuring outstanding American and international artists. Venues ranged from the Palace Saloon (Beer and G-Strings) to local churches, the courthouse and even Fort Clinch. **The Ritz-Carlton** hosted the final concert.

Amelia's Flags

Since Europeans arrived in 1762, Amelia Island has flown eight flags – French (1562-1565), Spanish (1565-1763 and 1783-1821), British (1763-1783), Patriots (1812), Green Cross of Florida (1817), Mexican (1817), Confederate (1861-1862) and U.S. (1862-?).

Jacksonville Beach

Jacksonville Beach is a pleasant corner of Florida. It's neither as historic as Fernandina and St. Augustine, nor as glitzy as Jacksonville, nor as upscale as Amelia and Ponte Verda. And therein lies its charm.

If, like us, your sense of adventure is on hold after a rigorous drive from Canada, just turn east from I-75 or I-95 and stop when you get to the ocean. Quiet beaches, moderate weather, affordable food and accommodation await.

Kayak Adventures, of Jacksonville Beach ☎ *904-249-6200* ☻ *www.kayakadventuresllc.com*

Kayaking is a growing pastime throughout Florida, and Walt Bunso, an award-winning kayaker and teacher, shares the enthusiasm. His company,

Kayak Adventures of Jacksonville Beach offers open water kayak instruction, rentals and guiding. Half and full-day trips explore the Intracoastal Waterway, penetrating to the remote wilderness of the barrier islands and their state parks.

Walt has created the Disabled Paddlers Association which sponsors free workshops to introduce disabled folks and their families to kayaking. His success stories include a quadriplegic person who needed foam wedges to remain upright in the kayak. "I work with their abilities, not their disabilities," Walt explained. Overcoming their fear is the first challenging step.

Kayak guiding and instruction – including workshops for disabled paddlers – are offered by Walt Bunso.

The Comfort Inn Oceanfront ✪ *1515 North 1st St., Jacksonville Beach* ✪ *1-800-654-8776* ✪ *www.comfortinnjaxbeach.com*

The Comfort Inn afforded no surprises – just a quiet, well appointed room overlooking the ocean, a pleasant breakfast, and super-helpful staff who pointed us toward all the area's best restaurants and attractions. Outside, there's a spacious 105-degree spa and a 120-foot heated serpentine pool, ringed by four waterfalls that tumble merrily over tall rocks, all just steps away from an uncrowded white sand beach. And for people with disabilities 15 of the 177 rooms are fully accessible, complete with roll-in showers.

Mayport

An American naval base sprawls along the ocean-front at Mayport, a tiny village at the mouth of the St. John River, north of Jacksonville Beach. Accessible through the naval station is a handsome red 1859 lighthouse, which saw active duty when union gunboats laid siege to Jacksonville during the Civil War. It contains paintings, scale models of lighthouses, rare photos and navigational aids. **The Mayport Ferry** is just down the road. (Every 30 minutes, 6 am-10 pm $2.75 for private cars.)

Mayport's second and major attraction is seafood so fresh that it's worth the drive from Canada! Shrimp fishing has been an important industry here for a century or more. The harbour is full of picturesque shrimp boats and the dock is lined with weather-beaten shacks selling shrimp and other seafood, both raw and cooked.

Singleton's Seafood Shack ✪ *($-$$)* ✪ *4728 Ocean St., Mayport 32233* ✪ *904-246-4442 (Open daily, year-round, lunch and dinner.)*

Our only regret about Singleton's is that we can't return sooner. The chowder was thick and succulent, the shrimp lightly spiced and crunchy, the service friendly, the prices moderate. The view of the harbour with its fishing boats, and closer-up, just outside the screened verandah, the hungry pelicans eyeing our every bite, made for awesome scenery.

This family business, begun by Ray Singleton, is now operated by his wife, Ann, whose paintings adorn the walls, and their son, Dean. An amateur wood carver, Ray faced blindness late in life, but that didn't prevent him from producing dozens of model wooden boats – from a foot-long dinghy to a four-foot shrimp boat and an elaborate paddle wheeler. They're all displayed – but none are for sale – in a museum off the main dining room. A prominent sign states: "Unattended children will be sold as slaves."

Slave cabins, dating from about 1800, recall history of slavery at Kingsley Plantation near Jacksonville.

Fort George, Little and Big Talbot Islands

Kingsley Plantation
✪ *Hwy. 11676 Palmetto Ave., Fort George Island. (Follow signs from Mayport Ferry landing.)*
✪ *904- 251-3537*
✪ *(Free adm. Daily 9-5.)*

The history of slavery and freedom are encapsulated in the Kingsley Plantation on Fort George Island, the first of three barrier islands north of the Mayport ferry. The coquina walls of slave cabins still stand, encircling the fine plantation house, which dates from about 1800. Here lived

Zephaniah Kingsley and his wife, Anna Madgigine Jai, a Senegal-born slave who was freed by her husband and proved herself courageous in the face of persecution and competent in the ways of management and finance.

Exhibits and artifacts trace the history of slavery in Florida – ricocheting between the Spaniards' fairly liberal attitude toward race and U.S. oppression and inhumanity. Sea Island cotton, the plantation's principal crop, grows in the garden. Interpretive programs are staged in the barn, built of an oyster-shell concrete called tabby. The 23 slave cabins, one of them restored to its original state, are chilling reminders of the past.

Orphaned and injured birds are nursed back to health at BEAKS.

BEAKS, 12084 Houston Ave., Big Talbot Island, FL 32226. ☎ 904-251-2473. www.beaks.org ✿ Open Tuesday to Sunday, 12-4.

Board the car ferry in **Mayport**, chug across the St. John River and drive through the wilderness of Little Talbot Island to **Big Talbot Island**. There you'll find a unique wildlife centre – and maybe a job to do.

This is **BEAKS – the Bird Emergency Aid and Kare Sanctuary**, which rescues and rehabilitates injured wildlife. The centre receives around 2,000 birds each year – from eagles and wood storks to blue jays and wrens, plus plenty of pelicans – victims of shootings, poisonings, car collisions or simply lost habitat. Most of them return to the wild after treatment.

Wildlife pays a high price for Florida's development, escalating workloads for the sanctuary, which relies entirely on donations. So visitors are welcome – and financial help is gratefully received.

But this is no theme park where cute trained animals perform tricks. It's a forest wilderness with make-shift facilities, where founders Cindy Mosling and Andrew Liliskis, along with every volunteer they can find, labour 'round the clock.

And speaking of **volunteers**, visitors can lend a hand at BEAKS. Cindy and her colleagues provide training in essential jobs such as preparing food or, in the spring, feeding voracious orphaned babies. And an oil spill or comparable disaster needs volunteers to rescue and clean birds whose lives depend upon swift action. Whether you have a day, a week or more, contact Cindy and pitch in. There's always more than enough work to go around. Volunteers attend to their own accommodations in nearby Jacksonville or Jacksonville Beach.

BEAKS is expanding its facilities and programs with a reception centre and emergency hospital with examination rooms, X-ray and labs. Plans are also afoot for a nature camp where visitors can spend a week enjoying the wilderness and working with the birds.

Jacksonville

Jacksonville folks like to point out that their city surpassed 100,000 in population a century ago, when Miami was little more than a swamp.

Close to Georgia and similar in its gracious and hospitable demeanour, Jacksonville is awash in shopping and restaurants, especially at Jacksonville Landing, an upscale riverfront marketplace. The winter months sparkle with theatre, music and literary events. For visitors who can't survive without theme parks, it's just a couple of hours north of Orlando.

Much Ado About Books ❂ *904-630-1995* ❂ *www.muchadoabout-books. com* ❂ is a day-long book fest in mid-February, at the **Prime Osborn Convention Center**, a building that preserves the century-old

Time to unwind – a comfy rocking chair, a seascape and Elizabeth Pointe Lodge hospitality.

Jacksonville Railway Station and even has a steam engine in its parking lot. Letting off steam inside are some three dozen authors, who meet, greet and autograph all day long. A literary luncheon ($25 or, for seating with an author, $40) and a gala dinner and silent auction ($100) wrap up the day, with proceeds to the Public Library and Library Foundation. The Convention Center is handy to the Skyway Express, a monorail system that whisks you around downtown Jacksonville.

Theatre flourishes, especially in winter. **The Florida Theatre** (*128 Forsyth St.* ☎ *904-355-ARTS. www.floridatheatre.com*), a restored 1920s movie palace, presents some 300 shows annually, from light opera to Irish dance. **The Florida Community College and Nathan H. Wilson Center for the Performing Arts,** (*11901 Beach Blvd.* ☎ *904-646-2349*) mounts a winter-long roster of concerts, photography and art shows, even Shakespeare.

Italian and English gardens surround the **Cummer Museum of Art**, (*829 Riverside Avenue – Riverside* ☎ *904 - 356-6857, www.cummer.org*) whose collection covers western art from 2000 BC to the present.

The Alhambra Dinner Theatre, (*12000 Beach Blvd.* ☎ *904- 641-1212, www.alhambradinnertheatre.com*) has been performing Broadway-style musicals and comedies for three decades. The shows – recent editions included La Cage aux Folles and Grease – are staged in a 400-seat theatre, following a generous dinner buffet.

Anheuser-Busch Brewery, (*111 Busch Dr.* ☎ *904-751-8117, www.budweisertours.com*) offers daily tours to view the brewing and packaging process and sample free beer.

Greyhound racing (904 - 646-0001) is offered by three separate kennels – Jacksonville Kennel Club (live racing April-October), Orange Park Kennel Club (live racing Oct.-April), and St. Johns Greyhound Racing Park (simulcast racing only). www.jaxkennel.com

Phone numbers

Although many Florida inns advertise toll-free numbers, very few extend that courtesy to Canadians. As well, the state's telephone area codes are changing. We've done our best to provide current numbers, but these two factors may result in calls that can't be completed. Do remind innkeepers that Canadians comprise a huge market in Florida and the courtesy of a toll-free number is simply good business.

Right down the middle
Ocala to Orlando

Canadians intent on theme parks and beaches tend to blast straight down I-75 or I-95, bypassing some of Florida's most appealing attractions. But hit the brakes at Ocala, an hour or so north of Orlando, and you're in the midst of quaint villages, mighty forests and lakes and picture-perfect countryside populated by the some of the world's finest horses.

This region's rich native culture ended abruptly with the arrival of Europeans, bearing their gifts of war, disease and greed. The local Timucuan Indians were wiped out by the mid-1700s and the two Seminole Indian wars of the early 1800s destroyed any remaining native presence. In the later 1800s, the citrus industry flourished and Ocala blossomed into one of the state's largest towns while nearby Silver Springs became an international tourist attraction with visitors arriving by steamboat. Finally, in 1935, the first Thoroughbred farm was founded and today that industry generates about $1 billion a year.

Ocala

Ocala is horse country. It seems that everybody in town and countryside loves, drives or rides magnificent steeds of every breed, from gentle giant Percherons and fluffy-footed Clydesdales to handsome Morgans –

When Horse Fever gripped Ocala, the event generated 53 hand-painted fantasies that raised $847,000 in a charity auction. Equine events dot the calendar year-round.

Like everyone in Ocala, Mary Garland loves horses, especially gentle Bill, who pulls her carriages.

the mount of choice for the local police – to hunters and carriage horses. We met Irish draught horses, elegant quarter horses and Thoroughbreds, and some new-to-us breeds as well. Many a Queen's Plate and Derby winner originated here and graze in these green pastures, shaded by towering moss-covered live oaks. In fact, the US Department of Agriculture (no doubt after world-wide consultation), named Ocala **'Horse Capital of the World.'**

So beloved are Ocala's horses that when Toronto was blocking its sidewalks with life-size moose, (all promptly relieved of their antlers except, for some reason, the one facing the police station), Ocala offered horses to be decorated by local artists and sponsored by local businesses. This fabulous herd was later auctioned off, raising $847,000 for charity, half to the bidder's favourite, half to the Marion County Art Alliance which funds community arts projects. And when you drive in or around Ocala, you'll still see some of those life-size equestrian statues, in all their fantastical and colourful glory.

Equestrian events large and small – rodeos, horse shows, rides and rallies – dot the Ocala calendar. One of North America's biggest hunter/jumper shows, the five-week **Horses in the Sun** (HITS) event, happens each spring in Ocala.

Ocala Carriage and Tours ☼ *1-877-996-2252* ☼ *www.OcalaTours.com*

Mary Garland has her finger on the equine pulse of Ocala. When she abandoned Maine for Marion County five years ago, she swapped horse-

What better way to pass an afternoon than a carriage ride along Ocala's pleasant byways, shaded by towering live oaks.

drawn sleigh rides (chilly!) for country carriage rides (bliss!), clip-clop-ping along behind Bill, a massive Clydesdale, who stops frequently to commune with his many equine friends at horse farms by the road-side. Mary offers carriage tours of all kinds – from old-style trolleys drawn by hefty draught horses, (she has both Percherons and Clydesdales) to elegant wedding tours. Her snow-white wedding carriage, uphol-stered in bur-gundy and decked with flowers and lights, is drawn by Mick and Mack, gleaming black twin Percherons. Her wagons are made in Canada – at the Roberts & Fils Carriage Works in St. Pie, Que. In fact she's Florida distributor for the Roberts line of carriages.

Through her own **Ocala Tours**, Mary provides a full travel service for her area – flights, accommodation, tours and of course weddings. She'll not only transport wedding couples in style, she'll set up an entire wedding complete with chapel or a fabulous nature site, officiating clergy, even the reception. On her own 40-acre property just outside Ocala, she recently organized a rustic wedding with hay bales for guest seating, a gazebo for the ceremony. At the elegant end of the spectrum, she may book the upscale **Jumbolair Estate** or the **Rosslar Manor** (see below).

Seven Sisters Inn ✿ *($$)* ✿ *820 Fort King St., Ocala* ✿ *352-867-1170*
✿ *www.7sistersinn.com*

Seven Sisters is a fantastical place – two places really, because it spans two adjoining Queen Anne houses in Ocala's historic district. The exteriors, wondrously pastel painted in sky blue with pink, green and golden yellow accents. conjure a fairy-tale image. And in the antique and curio-laden interior, your heart goes out to the cleaning staff, charged with keeping the dust off clocks and plastic palm trees, antique telephones and typewriters, rocking horses and gilded picture frames, teddy bears and Oriental woven baskets, china, glass, bamboo, fabric, wood, wicker and fine Oriental rugs, to name just some.

Our main floor room was decorated in gold-tossed red walls, with a four poster bed like a football field draped in zebra patterned fabric, with herds of jungle animals smiling back from pillows and throws. A bright red two-person whirlpool tub beckoned from the bathroom along with two shiny black sinks plus a shower.

There was afternoon tea with cakes and cheese, and best of all, because it was a Saturday, a murder mystery evening that continued from pre-dinner drinks through a full-course dinner. A successful murder mystery evening depends upon both guests and host letting down their hair and giving vent to their acting and sleuthing skills. On that occasion, much hair, some of it fright wigs, was let down and the acting and sleuthing skills were worthy of a Gemini. The upstairs costume room, with a Tickle Trunk that Mr. Dressup would have applauded, contributed to the fun. The hats were to die for.

Listed on the National Register of Historic Places, the inn has 13

The historic Seven Sisters Inn is a Queen Anne style mansion packed with curios and antiques.

Horses and art share the spotlight at Rosslor Manor outside Ocala.

guest rooms, each with huge canopy or wrought iron beds, fireplaces, soaking tubs and fascinating antiques. Smoking, children under 12 and pets are not accommodated. Breakfast and afternoon tea are included in the rates.

Rosslor Manor ✪ *($$$-$$$$)*
✪ *P.O. Box 687, Silver Springs 34489*
✪ *352-236-4219*
✪ *www.rosslor.com*

In the countryside near Silver Springs, just east of Ocala, sits a luxurious B&B where riders can hone their skills or simply ride the trails and relax. Hosts Rich and Laurie Ross extend warm hospitality in a luxurious setting. Rich, a professional musician and one-time Vancouver resident, toured Canada with the **Ducette** rock band. (Remember 'Mamma don't dance'?) Loryn was a Judicial Commissioner in California – she's licensed to perform marriage ceremonies and their handsome manor house and picturesque grounds, where a cathedral-arch of live oaks leads to a picturesque gazebo, form the perfect backdrop.

Set within a 50-acre estate, the two-story house is approached by a broad driveway that encircles a huge fountain. Inside three sumptuously appointed guest rooms, two with king size beds, one with twin beds and optional cot, provide creature comforts. Downstairs, there's a wood-burning fireplace, a grand piano and deep couches, plus billiards in the games room. A stick-to-the-ribs breakfast starts the day and you can also order (in advance) a gourmet picnic lunch.

The fenced paddocks are home to a family of interesting horses – dappled Irish draughts, a Quarterhorse/Arab, a Trekehner, and Peruvian Pasos. But with private paddocks and secure stalls in the handsome stables, some visitors prefer to bring their own mounts, especially if they're seeking advanced training in dressage or jumping, both available at Rosslor. In fact, there's riding instruction for every level of skill, from beginner to advanced and plenty of hiking trails both on the estate and in the surrounding countryside.

Two bright-eyed Maltese terriers, a Peke named Foufie, a gaggle of cats and a pot-bellied pig called Paddy assist with the hosting. The property includes a one-acre pond for swimming and fishing.

Jumbolair Inn and Country Club ✪ *($$$-$$$$)* ✪ *1201 NE 77th Street, Ocala 34479* ✪ *352-401-1990* ✪ *www.jumbolair.com*

A private and exclusive enclave – literally for the jet-set – is **Jumbolair Inn and Country Club**, a gated estate just north of Ocala. It boasts the world's largest FAA licensed, lighted and paved private airstrip – 7,550 feet – with a 10-acre paved parking pad.

Ocala is on line at accessocala.com

Jumbolair's luxurious bed and breakfast inn will soon be joined by an upscale housing development, **Jumbolair Aviation Estates**, where every home comes with its own aircraft hanger.

The inn, situated deep within woods and paddocks, offers five guest rooms, furnished in antiques and fine art. The rate includes full breakfast, use of an extensive fitness centre, outdoor pool, games room with billiards and parking for car or plane. For horse fans, an equestrian facility is set within hundreds of acres of trails. Adjacent to the inn is a smartly appointed meeting room which is also a favourite spot for wedding receptions.

Ritz Historic Inn ✪ *1205 Silver Springs Blvd.* ✪ *($$)* ✪ *Ocala* ✪ *1-888 382-9390* ✪ *www.ritzhistoric-inn.com*

Back in town, you can hobnob with the rich and famous – or at least vivid memories of them – at **The Ritz Historic Inn**. A grand old hotel built in 1925, it did time as an apart-

From Katherine Hepburn to Tarzan, many big names have visited the historic Ritz Inn.

Every breed of horse is likely found in Ocala. The police department's mounts are sturdy Morgans.

ment complex, half-way house and homeless shelter, before its recent transformation into 35 spacious and interesting suites at affordable prices. We especially liked the Spanish suite which consisted of sitting room, king-size bedroom, a bathroom big enough to throw a party, and a spacious balcony. Each room contains a refrigerator and microwave. Breakfast is a deluxe continental, often served beside the pool. There's live jazz on Friday evenings and karaoke on Wednesdays. The gardens and reception rooms are favourite venues for weddings and receptions.

The Ritz has played host to some big names in its time, including Lloyd Bridges, Katherine Hepburn and Spencer Tracey, John Travolta and Johnny Weismuller, who filmed several Tarzan movies in the area.

Good Eats...

Ocala abounds with eateries in every price range. Here's a sampling.

Hightowers Seafood and Steaks ❂ *($$)* ❂ *754 N.E. 25th Ave.* ❂ *352-622-8220* ❂ specializes in seafood – lobster, crab, clams, shrimps, scallops and more – but you'll also find steaks of many persuasions, chicken and pasta, plus Key lime or peanut butter pie. Open for lunch and dinner.

Carmichael's ❂ *($$)* ❂ *3105 N.E. Silver Springs Blvd.* ❂ *352-622-3636* offers a mid-price menu ranging from prime rib to seafood to pasta plus 'lite' dishes such as a vegetable paella or a seasonal fruit plate. Lunch features a lengthy list of sandwiches and salads.

Museums and Galleries

Appleton Museum of Art (Florida State University and Central Florida Community College) ✪ *4333 NE Silver Springs Blvd., Ocala 34478-3190* ✪ *352-236-7100* ✪ *www.appletonmuseum.org*

Too often overlooked at home, Canadian art stars in many a show in Ocala. The splendid **Appleton Museum of Art** is headed by Canadian Jeffrey Spaulding. In his first two years with the institution, Spaulding

Even the horses are friendly in Ocala. Friendly Bill, a huge Percheron, pauses for a chat with the youngsters.

introduced Ocala to Canadian art big-time with exhibitions of the works of Emily Carr, and major collections of 19th and 20th century works from the **Art Gallery of Ontario** (AGO). Already repository of a solid but staid collection of European old masters, the Appleton's galleries house a fabulous collection of pre-Columbian artifacts, an absorbing exhibition of 1930s photographs of the Miccosukee Indians of the Florida Everglades, a fine set of Mediaeval illuminated manuscripts and contemporary works by Florida and other artists. A recent show, Speak Softly and Carry a Beagle, featured the art of Charles Schultz, of Peanuts cartoon fame.

The Appleton has a long history with Canada since Dr. Roald Nasgaard, curator of contemporary art at the AGO, and later head of the art department at Florida State University, curated shows there, garnering support from many of the AGO's patrons and board members who maintain winter homes in Florida.

Silver Springs, Ocala National Forest

The museum offers many peripheral delights such as concerts, video presentations, lectures and informative tours. There's an excellent gift shop and a pleasant café for light lunches.

The Marion County Museum of History ✪ *307 SE 26th Terrace* ✪ *352-629-2773* ✪ recalls early life in the area with artifacts and memorabilia that include a Seminole Indian camp and clothing, a 1,500-year-old canoe found locally, photo histories and an old homestead model.

Silver River Museum and Environmental Education Center ✪ *Silver River State Park, 1425 NE 58th Avenue* ✪ *352-236-7148* ✪ showcases Florida history, natural history, geology, archaeology, paleontology and ecology and there's a replica of an old Florida 'cracker' village. A boardwalk leads down to the river, affording views of the natural environment.

Silver Springs, Nature's Theme Park and Wild Waters Park ✪ *5656 East Silver Springs Blvd., Silver Springs 34488* ✪ *352-236-2121* ✪ *www.silversprings.com* ✪ *wildwaterspark.com*

Billed as Florida's oldest theme park, **Silver Springs** is next door to Ocala. The attraction dates back to 1878 when the first glass-bottomed boat was unveiled. That boat ride is still the park's most popular attraction, providing wondrous views of aquatic life and fossils, deep in the crystal-clear waters of the spring which pours 550 million gallons of water into the river each day.

At Silver Springs, an attraction since 1878, popular glass-bottomed boats reveal aquatic life and fossils.

The park radiates an air of old-fashioned elegance and dignity. Yet it's far from stuffy or dull. Smooth walkways criss-cross its 350 acres, dotted with quaint pavilions and stores, flowers, fabulous topiary animals and fountains. Classical music drifts from the public address system. Pleasant outdoor eateries serve affordable food – for example, a vast submarine sandwich loaded with tuna or chicken and salad greens for $5.95. Children wrestle with oversized ice cream cones.

Jungle cruises and jeep safaris venture deep into the wilderness. Animal shows (from 'gator wrangling to snakes to birds of prey), a petting zoo and a solid line-up of concerts – 22 of them in one three-month span, from jazz to country to R&B – feature the likes of **Anne Murray, Wayne Newton** and the **Smothers Brothers**. Admission prices include the shows.

If you love horses, you'll love Ocala where some of the world's finest horses graze in rolling green pastures.

A Native American Festival in November, and December's sparkling Festival of Lights round out the year. And for a few extra dollars, you can include the nine-acre **Wild Waters Park** next door, with water slides, flumes and pools, plus a 450,000-gallon wave pool and deck chairs that encourage parents to unwind while keeping an eye on the tads.

Silver Springs is open year-round, rain or shine. Wild Waters is open March to September with various hours and days. (Consult website calendars.) The parks are on S.R. 40, off I-75, just east of Ocala. Silver Springs one-day admission (all rides, concerts, shows and special events), $32.99; seniors, $29.99, folks under 48 inches, $23.99; two and under, free. Season pass for both facilities: $49.99, seniors, 55 or better, $35.99 (also includes all shows, concerts, etc.)

Ocala National Forest

Ocala National Forest ✪ *352-236-0288* ✪ *www.onf.net* ✪ was decimated by a forest fire in 1999, probably started by a sloppy smoker's discarded butt. The blackened stumps are a sad sight, visible from Highways 19 and 314 (this last branching off to Ocala to the west) which

Incitement to relax – rockers and wilderness at Ocklawaha.

traverse the park. But beyond the burn, there's still plenty of forest – 383,000 acres to be exact – **the Florida National Scenic Trail** and many other smaller trails, several spectacular springs and recreation areas and hundreds of camping sites, from rustic to full-service.

The Refuge at Ocklawaha ✪ *($)* ✪ *14835 South East 85th Street, Ocklawaha 32179* ✪ *352- 288-2233* ✪ *www.floridarefuge.org*

At the southwest corner of the **Ocala National Forest**, there's a hidden gem – the Refuge at Ocklawaha, operated by **Central Florida YMCA**. This 52-acre paradise is 10 miles from the village but an eternity away from the hustle and bustle of civilization. The 23 tin-roofed cabins, set far apart amongst tall oaks and shrubbery, issue urgent invitations to relax in rocking chairs on screened porches. Accommodating up to four people, the cottages are comfortable but not fancy. They have private baths, ceiling fans, a small refrigerator for drinks and snacks. Breakfast is available at $3 per person, hearty lunches at $7.50 or $3.25 for kids, a complete dinner for $12, $6 for kids, all served at the main lodge, a converted rancher's house. YMCA members get a special rate for cabins – 2002 rates were $90 for members, $110 for non-members.

Bikes are available to guests free of charge and there are miles of hiking and biking trails. Canoes can be rented ($15 per day) to explore the Ocklawaha River and horseback tours are available ($30 for about an hour). There's also a short nature trail, offering a mini-education in the flora and fauna of the area, which is adjacent to the 4,400-acre **Ocklawaha Restoration Area**. Bird watching, butterfly netting, and 'owl prowls' are among organized activities.

Continental Acres Equine Resort ❂ *3000 Marion County Road,
Weirsdale.* ❂ *352-750-5500* ❂ *www.continentalacres.com* ❂ *Tours
(reservations required), Tues-Sat. 2 p.m., year-round. Adm.: $10.*

Three attractions in one, this 365-acre farm at Weirsdale, south-east of
Ocala, offers carriage and coaching lessons, dressage rings and cones
courses to weekly, monthly or winter-long guests. The 39,000-sq.-ft.
Austin Carriage Museum (352-750-1763) houses a collection of 136
century-old horse-drawn carriages, most of them driven in competitions
around the world by owner Gloria Austin.

A life-long equestrian, Ms. Austin fell in love with carriage driving after
observing classes at the **Royal Winter Fair** in Toronto. Her collection
includes a medicine carriage, a mail buggy and a large hunting carriage
with a compartment for dogs. Tours at 2 p.m., Tues-Fri. Adm: $10.

The Austin Education Center (352-750-1417 ❂ www.austineducation-
center.com) offers workshops for horse enthusiasts of various disciplines,
but also brings the "non-horse person" reasonably priced workshops on
equine-related subjects such as the history of the horse and horses in
warfare. The Center also hosts **Elderhostel** programs spring and fall.
A carriage festival demonstrates historic carriage driving, horse acts and
performances, the second Saturday of December.

Showcase of Citrus ❂ *Hwy. 27, Clermont.* ❂ *1-800-224-8787*
❂ *www.showcaseofcitrus.com*

The Showcase of Citrus near Clermont introduces visitors to the rural
Florida of days gone by and to the citrus industry that continues to
flourish here.

Owner John Arnold, who grew up on this 2,500-acre working citrus
grove and cattle ranch, now offers **Outback Wild Adventure Tours** in a
monster yellow-and-black, tiger-striped swamp buggy. Visitors tour
marshlands, shallow lakes, prairies, woods and pasture lands, to spy
deer, wild pigs, foxes, raccoons, alligators, possums, armadillos, coyotes,
wild turkey and various migratory and wetland birds. The property is also
home to the largest flock of wild scarlet macaw parrots in North America.
But it's the citrus grove that's the heart of the matter. More than 50 varieties of citrus grow here and visitors can sample fresh fruit straight from
the trees as they tour the groves. Open daily, October to May. Tours by
appointment Wed. and Sat, $20.

Orlando

Lovely lakes and flowery parklands prove there are more reasons than theme parks to visit Orlando.

Orlando – The city we love to ignore

Hardly anybody visits Orlando. Although more than half a million Canadians fly into Orlando each year, the majority scoot on out to the theme parks, thus abandoning a pleasant reality for a pricey fantasy.

If major theme parks are not your prime vacation choice, join the club. And leave time for a look at the real Orlando.

Like many American cities, Orlando fell victim to cars and super high-ways, which suck the life out of downtown in favour of the suburbs.

Yet downtown Orlando has much to offer – a landscape dotted with beautiful lakes, a 'cultural corridor' of museums and galleries, some fine, though expensive, hotels, and a bit of night life. In fact, valiant efforts are underway to resuscitate the downtown core, in particular the **Church Street Station**, a fine old train station that for a while, was a hub of bustling activity. Now in the hands of new developers, it's sparkling again. Recent arrivals include the **Orlando Black Essential Theatre**, an African-American company, the **Orlando Youth Theatre**, a children's company and **Louis' Downtown Restaurant**, noted for Southern home cooking.

Because the huge Canadian market has weakened in recent years, Orlando and its major players make special efforts to woo Canadians with discounts and deals. The programs may change– best to check them out at www.orlandokissimmee.com/canada.

Two money-savers that seem likely to survive are the **Orlando Magicard**, with discounts from about 100 local businesses, and the **Mature Travelers Guide** for 55-plus folks, with deals at 50 establishments. Request at 1-800-551-0181, www.orlandoinfo.com or at the **Visitor Center**, 8723 International Driver, (9-7 daily except Christmas).

The car is king in Orlando and public transportation is substandard. There's a public bus service, plus Lymmo buses which provide limited – but free – service in the downtown area. Even taxis can be hard to find downtown, since their big business is between airport and resort hotels.

To See and Do . . .

Morse Museum ❁ 445 Park Ave. N., Winter Park 32789 ❁ 407-645-5311 ❁ www.morsemuseum.org

Louis Comfort Tiffany is a familiar name. But few realize the extent and genius of his art. Although we associate him with colourful lamps and a New York jewelry shop, Tiffany turned his hand to almost every medium – stained and blown glass, pottery, metalwork, enamels and jewelry. Trained as a painter, he began, at 24, to study the chemistry and techniques of glassmaking, developing his unique opalescent glass in which colours were combined and manipulated to create three-dimensional effects. His work was wildly popular and there was scarcely a fine house in America that did not boast a Tiffany window or panel. His greatest work was undoubtedly the **Tiffany Chapel**, created for the Chicago World's Fair in 1893.

Tiffany built an 84-room mansion, Laurelton Hall, on a 580-acre country estate on Long Island, in 1902. He died in 1933 and although he created an endowment fund to maintain the estate, the money ran out and in 1946 the house contents were auctioned. In 1957, fire gutted the house, now long abandoned, apparently destroying the magnificent works that Tiffany had incorporated into the design

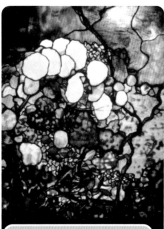

The genius of Tiffany is displayed at the Morse Museum.

Tiffany's splendid Chapel, created in 1893, was saved from destruction by Morse Museum founders.

and interior décor.

Into the charred ruins stepped Jeannette Genius McKean and her husband, Hugh F. McKean, both Tiffany admirers, who rashly offered $10,000 for salvage rights to what was left, none of it considered worth saving. But the nay-sayers were wrong. It was very much worth saving and the **Charles Hosmer Morse Museum of American Art** (named for Mrs. McKean's grandfather) is a brilliant and absorbing testimonial to the vision of the McKeans and the genius of Tiffany.

At its heart is the magnificent Byzantine-inspired Chapel, now carefully restored, a fantasy of stained and leaded glass, mosaics, columns and arches. The Chapel had fallen upon hard times. After the World's Fair, it was purchased by a wealthy donor for the Episcopal Cathedral Church of St. John the Divine in New York. There it was relegated to the basement where it suffered extensive water damage before Tiffany rescued and repaired it, installing it at his Long Island estate. After his death, however, it was dismantled and sold off in bits and pieces.

The McKeans salvaged what remained, then set about tracking down the missing furnishings. Finally, the massive restoration project was completed. **The Tiffany Chapel**, deep within the Morse Museum, is surely worth the trip to **Winter Park.**

The museum's displays constitute the largest collection of Tiffany's work and encompass all of his artistry – glass, pottery, enamels, jewelry and an absorbing photographic display of his estate before and after the fire. The excellent gift shop sells Tiffany reproductions and much more.

The museum is open Tues – Sat, 9:30 to 4. Closed on major public holidays. Adm: Adults $3, students $1, children under 12 free. Free admission Fridays, 4 to 8, Sept.-May.

Nature Conservancy's Disney Wilderness Preserve ✪ *2799 Scrub Jay Trail, Kissimmee 34759* ✪ *407-935-0002* ✪ *www.nature.org/florida* ✪ *Open daily 9-5.*

Forget the furry robots. Have a look at the real thing.

The Nature Conservancy offers raw reality at its 12,000-acre preserve, home to hundreds of wildlife species. Hiking trails, buggy tours and guided walks reveal the preserve's resident plants and animals and efforts to restore and protect them.

If you're a long-stay Florida visitor, you can even volunteer – as a tour guide or part of the wildlife monitoring program. Volunteers attend an eight-week training course and work as their time permits during winter months. The monitoring program runs January to April and keeps tabs on wood storks, Florida sandhill cranes, gopher tortoises, and Florida scrub jays.

The Nature Conservancy maintains three other locations in Florida, all eager for both visitors and volunteers. Check them out at www.nature.org/florida.

Downtown Orlando, with its pleasant vistas, good restaurants and fine lodgings, may be making a comeback.

Titanic – The Exhibition ✪ *8445 International Drive, Orlando 32819* ✪ *Open 10-9 daily. Adm: Adults, $16.95, children 6-12, $11.95; kids under 6, free.*

The Titanic may have floundered nearly a century ago, but it lives on in Orlando. This exhibition sets out to recreate both the physical and the emotional aspects of the great ship, drawing on the movies for some of its artifacts and inspiration. Actors depicting passengers and crew lead tours every half hour.

Gardens

Orlando is endowed with several delightful gardens. Especially interesting are the **Harry P. Leu Gardens** which include a splendid camellia garden and further out of town. For details – Gardens page 176.

And so to sleep . . .

Downtown Orlando boasts a few good B&Bs and some fine hotels.

The Courtyard at Lake Lucerne ✪ *($$-$$$)* ✪ *211 North Lucerne Circle E., Orlando 32801* ✪ *800-444-5289 or 407-648-5188* ✪ *info@orlandohistoricinn.com.*

This fine inn overlooking Lake Lucerne is walking distance from Orlando's downtown shopping and dining. Its four historic houses, each from a different era, encircle a lush tropical garden replete with fountains, flowers and benches. Guests are greeted with a complimentary carafe of wine, there's an afternoon cocktail hour and an excellent breakfast is included in the room rate. Restoring the old houses, the oldest dating from 1883, has been a painstaking labour of love for Charles Meiner, who likes to spend his summers in Montreal, scooping up all the antiques and collectibles that Canadians have not yet learned to appreciate. The houses are furnished and decorated with numerous treasures.

The Veranda Bed and Breakfast ✪ *($$-$$$)* ✪ *115 N. Summerlin Ave., Orlando 32801* ✪ *407-849-0321* ✪ *www.theverandabandb.com*

Here's another historic collection, this time in Thornton Park, near Lake Eola, an area of trendy shops and eateries. The five buildings date from the early 1900s and there's a garden courtyard for weddings and parties, a swimming pool and an extensive breakfast included in the room rate.

Westin Grand Bohemian ✪ *($$$-$$$$)* ✪ *325 S. Orange Ave., Orlando 32801* ✪ *1-888-GRAND123* ✪ *www.grandbohemianhotel.com*

Across the street from City Hall, walking distance from the best of downtown, this fine hotel, opened in 2001, is as much an art institution as a hostelry. Billed as 'An experience in art and music', the hotel's design was inspired by European Bohemia, now the Czech Republic, a hub of music and art. More than 100 works – oil paintings, glass, bronze and wood sculptures – decorate public areas, rest rooms and guest rooms and a main floor gallery sells original art. A $250,000 Grand Imperial Bosendorfer piano, one of only two in the world designed by Austrian architect Hans Hollien, provides nightly entertainment in the lounge. The main restaurant, The Boheme, ($$$) adds a dash of artwork, both to its décor and its menu, which groups its dishes musically – prelude, legato, leggiaro and accompanists. The hotel has an outdoor heated pool, fitness centre and business centre.

At Orlando Courtyard B&B, Charles Meiner displays his fine collection of Canadian-made chalet glass.

Climate-controlled bubble, the new Gaylord Palms Hotel caters to every possible luxury and taste.

Gaylord Palms Resort and Convention Center ✪ *($$$-$$$$)* ✪ *6000 W. Osceola Parkway, I-4, exit 26, Kissimmee, 34746.* ✪ *407-586-2000* ✪ *www.gaylord-palms.com*

Orlando is adept at creating fantasy and the Gaylord Palms is living proof. Beneath its 4.5 acre 364-foot glass atrium, are reproductions of historic St. Augustine, the Florida Keys and the Everglades. You can hike (on broad smooth paths) over lofty mini-mountains, past flower gardens, waterfalls and fog-enshrouded pools to a ring of nifty eateries and chic shops, leading to some 1,400 hotel rooms and a 400,000-square-foot convention space.

A full-service spa and fitness centre, swimming pools, including one with a humungous octopus waterslide, play areas, a children's day care, upscale shops and wandering entertainers – magicians, musicians, story tellers – are all part of the drama.

All those perks have their price ($400 to $480 in high season; dinner entrees from $27) but if your agenda calls for every possible luxury, infinite variety in activities, food and shopping, and a location just minutes from Orlando Airport and the theme parks, you've arrived.

Uncrowded beaches, untrammeled wilderness and myriad wildlife await visitors to the Titusville area, thanks to vast reserves set aside by NASA.

Titusville – Where everything flies

You could say that Titusville is strictly for the birds.

One of North America's great bird watching regions, Titusville and its sister communities in North Brevard County also boast a wealth of cultural icons – museums and historic sites, theatre, dance, music, festivals and family events, and of course the Kennedy Space Center.

So if it flies, chances are you'll find it in Titusville where birds and space shuttles compete for attention. The nearby Kennedy Space Center launches half a dozen or more spacecraft a year. And thanks to NASA, this vast area – some 140,000 acres of barrier islands – is protected, thus creating a sanctuary for a stunning variety of wildlife, especially birds. NASA knows a thing or two about the weather – hurricanes tend to pass by and the climate is temperate year-round.

Our guide to birdland was Nancy Evans, a passionate and knowledgeable birder. As sales manager for the Best Western Space Shuttle Inn, Nancy has turned her passion into a kind of house specialty, although as the name implies, space shuttles also have their place.

You may not consider a sewage treatment plant a highlight of your holiday but don't miss the Titusville Wetlands Reclamation Center, an award-winning facility that cuts the costs and environmental impact of water treatment, and incidentally provides sanctuary for both migrating and indigenous birds.

The town's sewage is processed to reduce sediment content, then filtered through ponds and plant life and returned for non-potable uses such as irrigating gardens and golf courses. The process is cheap, clean, efficient and above all natural. Its lavish plant life is both a result of and a contributor to the process. And the birds love it.

During our brief drive along the narrow berms that encircle the area, we spotted, with Nancy's help, flocks of American coots, blue-wing teal, Florida gallinule, redwing blackbirds, egrets, great white heron, ibis, tern, cormorants, loons, blue heron, anhinga, belted kingfishers and bittern. A remarkable sight was the 'heron condo' – a stand of cabbage palms, their foliage stomped down by the heron to make way for penthouse nests.

Proud but protective parents pay close attention to their family of fluffy chicks.

The water treatment plant is just the beginning of the Titusville/Space Coast birding bonanza. The Canaveral Seashore and Merritt Island Wildlife Refuge, both national parks, and many state-owned and community conservation areas are closely watched by a huge variety of nature conservancy organizations. In fact, the level of community involvement in maintaining and protecting wildlife sanctuaries is truly impressive.

Merritt Island National Wildlife Refuge ✪ *P.O. Box 6504, Titusville 32782* ✪ *Route 402 from north Titusville* ✪ *321-861-0667*

From mighty manatee to tiny birds, this 140,000-acre refuge, the second largest in Florida, provides sanctuary for myriad species. Peregrine falcon, gopher tortoises and eastern indigo snakes are among them. More than 400 manatee pay springtime visits to the North Banana River, joining over 500 species of wildlife seeking refuge in a perfect climate.

A six-mile self-guided driving tour and easy shaded boardwalks wind through pine and oak hammocks. At the Visitors Information Center, you'll find informative exhibits and literature, along with lectures and outdoor activities plus indefatigable volunteers helping with information, tours and maintenance.

Lining the seven-mile narrow gravel road leading to Black Point are thickets of cabbage palms, sand pines, scrub oak, palmettos and lagoons of black wire grass plus close-up encounters with birds, confident of their safety. We sighted vultures and hawks sailing overhead. Rosiate spoonbills and black neck stilts in their formal black and white outfits with bright red legs, were spectacular. White pelican occasionally are spotted here.

A small lagoon with a boat-launching dock attracts manatee. Though the water is brackish, it's believed that deep wells filter into the lagoon, providing the fresh water that manatee require. Despite motorized boat traffic, the huge beasts, many carting a cargo of barnacles on their black coats and every one of them scarred by past encounters with boat propellers, loiter near the surface, waiting to come up for air.

Canaveral National Seashore ✪ Route 402 from North Titusville ✪ 321-267-1110

The Canaveral Seashore access road passes only a mile or so from the launch pads of the Kennedy Center and spacecraft are clearly visible.

Heron condo is the local name for this collection of palmetto palms, their tops stomped flat by heron to make way for their spacious nests.

Several pull-offs that once allowed visitors to stop and observe the action are closed for security reasons and there's a security checkpoint at the main gate. The area is closed completely for a day or two before a launch.

Birding festivals are annual events in Titusville – and Canadians often walk off with top prizes

But the final nine parking areas are open. (Lot 7 provides wheelchair access to the beach, and a shade pavilion; clean restrooms are available at each parking lot.) Wooden stairs arc over the sand dunes (it's forbidden to walk on the dunes) and down to a fabulous beach – 24 miles of white sand with nary a high rise or fast food joint in sight. In fact, there was scarcely anything in sight during our weekday visit, except sand, sea, sky, shore birds and seabirds. But the isolation was deceptive. This is one of the largest sea turtle nesting areas in the U.S. From May to August, night-time guided tours let you witness loggerheads, green seas and leatherbacks coming ashore to lay their eggs.

Enchanted Forest Sanctuary ✪ North side of Route 405, 1/2 mile west of US Route 1, south of Titusville ✪ 321-267-7367

It was closed for renovations during our visit but Nancy assured us that The Enchanted Forest is an outstanding site with a pleasant variety of nature trails to suit all levels of energy and expertise. The 393-acre spread, protected under Brevard County's Environmentally Endangered Lands Program, commands enormous support from the community, which spearheaded its purchase back in the early nineties. An active volunteer group, Friends of the Enchanted Forest maintains programs and trails, and organizes nature walks. Open Wed. and Sat., 8:30-3:00, Sun. 2-5. An Earth Day Festival is a special event each April.

Space Coast Nature Tours aboard Skimmer ❖ Titusville Municipal Marina, Slip A23 ❖ 321-267-4551 ❖ www.spacecoastnaturetours.com

The Indian River Lagoon, all 160 miles of it, separates the barrier islands from the mainland. The lagoon and its islands – many of them man-made when the Intracoastal Waterway was dredged – are home to some 4,315 species of plants and animals, including the Florida manatee.

It's also home base for the 44-ft. pontoon vessel, the Skimmer, whose USCG licensed Captain, Ron Thorstad, is an enthusiastic booster for environmental initiatives. Fuelled by solar-powered batteries – silent and environmentally kind – the ship is fitted with rear propeller guards to protect both manatee and shallow water sea grasses. Wrapped in hand-made quilts to ward off fresh sea breezes and equipped with borrowed binoculars (though you're wise to bring your own), you're kept enter-tained and informed as Capt. Thorstad and on-board naturalists reveal the wild wonders of the lagoon. And thanks to an underwater micro-phone, you can eavesdrop on dolphin gossip – about 70 dolphin reside in the lagoon and they like to chat. Some 90 per cent of Florida clams are harvested here. White pelican are often sighted on Rookery Island and during our visit a pair of loons – rarely seen in southern Ontario – cruised the lagoon. During shuttle launches, Capt. Thorstad rolls back the roof to ensure a spectacular view.

The Kennedy Space Center, Visitor's Complex ❖ KSC, FL. 32899, south of Titusville, 5 miles east of Hwy. 1 ❖ 321-449-4444 ❖ www.kennedyspace-center.com

To experience all the wonders of the American Space Program, past, present and future, you need a full day. And to find information about current and future launches and ticket avail-

Two holidays in one – Kennedy Space Center plus great birding at Titusville.

Flora and fauna of Titusville area are depicted in colourful original mural painted – and regularly embellished – by local artist Al Rao.

ability, you also need plenty of time. These Space Center guys can put people on the moon but their website is a confusing tangle of broken links with obtuse and incomplete information.

At the Visitor Complex, a giant IMAX movie theatre introduces the space program and its history. You'll find exhibits of space history, a full-size walk-through space shuttle display and the new Apollo/Saturn V facility plus the Astronaut Hall of Fame, the Astronaut Memorial Planetarium and the Space Camp.

To see a launch, you can request a free car pass (far in advance) or buy a launch ticket at the Visitor Complex ($17.40). You can also watch the launch from various sites outside the Center – best to ask your hotel for suggestions unless you have hours to spend searching the KSC website.

Admission: Adult $26, child $16. Launch and admission packages: Adult $36.50, kids 3-11 $26.50.

Eating and sleeping ...

Dixie Crossroads Restaurant ✪ ($-$$) ✪ 1475 Garden St., Titusville 32796 ✪ 321-268-5000

Dixie Crossroads is a huge family-style restaurant, that specializes in fresh seafood but includes steak, prime rib and chicken on its extensive menu. At the helm is Capt. Laurilee Thompson, whose father Rodney, was a shrimp boat captain who developed the market for the hard-shelled rock shrimp.

The meal begins with warm sugar-dusted corn fritters. Save them for later or you won't have room for the succulent seafood – butterfly style rock shrimp, deep sea shrimp, scallops, crabs and lots of fish. A hearty meal of a dozen rock shrimp, half a dozen deep sea shrimps, half a dozen scallops, baked potato, salad and soup costs about $12.

The restaurant is built in the Florida cracker style with a tin roof, wood siding and shutters.

Outside, New York-born artist Al Rao has painted a vast and colourful mural depicting flora and fauna of the area.

Laurilee, a staunch supporter of Titusville's myriad birding and environmental initiatives, has created a garden that showcases native plants of Florida, accented by vividly blooming exotics, with a koi-stocked fish pond and butterfly garden The idea is to inspire homeowners to adapt their own yards to attract and nurture wildlife.

Birding Festivals

The Titusville area hosts various birding events including an April festival to 'welcome back the songbirds' and a five-day birding festival each November in which Canadians have shown a tendency to walk off with the top trophies. For additional information, contact Titusville and North Brevard County: www.nbbd.com

Kloiber's Cobbler Eatery ❂ ($) ❂ *337 S. Washington Ave., Titusville* ❂ *321-383-0689*

This big friendly three-story (plus patio) downtown dining spot serves breakfasts, lunches and dinners with 'no cans or cartons, no grilling or frying.' The broiled open-face breakfast sandwich 'will make you forget about eggs,' asserts manager Heidi Santti.

Quiche with fresh fruit (under $5) is a lunchtime special. But proprietors Pixie and Joe Kloiber have made fruit cobblers their specialty – fresh fruit in season – peaches, blueberries, strawberries, apples –with a hot biscuit topping, served with ice cream.

Lodgings

The best-known hotel chains have a major presence on the Space Coast.

Best Western Space Shuttle Inn ❂ *($$)* ❂ *3455 Cheney Hwy. (I-95 Exit #79), Titusville 32780* ❂ *1-800-523-7654* ❂ *www.spaceshuttleinn.com*

No fuss and few frills, Best Western provides affordable and comfortable accommodation in convenient locations and this hotel, just minutes from the Kennedy Space Center and some of the greatest birding in the world, is no exception. Spacious rooms, guest laundry, a heated outdoor pool and sauna, and an eco-fitness park with its own fishing lake are among the features. The rate includes continental breakfast and a Durango Steak House is part of the hotel. Best of all, there's plenty of expert advice on every possible attraction in the region, from birds to space shuttles.

Titusville and North Brevard County information: www.nbbd.com

Great Outdoors Golf and Nature Resort ❂ *($$-$$$)* ❂ *S.R. 50, west of I-95, exit 79* ❂ *1-800-621-2267* ❂ *www.tgoresort.com*

The Great Outdoors is a full-scale community for golfers. Although the amenities are plentiful and luxurious, prices are surprisingly affordable. There are luxury chalets and RV sites (18-ft. or more), a café, grocery store, pro shop, pub, pool and a good, affordable restaurant, the Plantation on the Green. An interdenominational church chimes sublimely on the hour.

The colonnaded Plantation House, popular for high school proms or wedding receptions, hosts a weekly (in season) social, Fridays, 5 to 7, to which everyone's invited.

On down the road

Florida Solar Energy Center ❂ *1679 Clearlake Road, Cocoa* ❂ *321-638-1000* ❂ *www.fsec.ucf.edu*

Solar energy, the untapped resource that could resolve many of the world's energy problems, is explored in depth at this 16-acre University of Central Florida research institute, where solar energy devices are tested and evaluated. The library contains thousands of books and documents.

Daytona Beach – speed up to slow down

Daytona Beach isn't exactly off the beaten track. It's been a hot tourist destination for well over a century and thousands of Canadians flock there every winter. But if you're looking for something weird and wacky, welcome to Daytona.

Our arrival coincided with the end of Bike Week and the beginning of School Break Week. Warning: It is challenging (but interesting) to visit Daytona Beach during this time slot. While hundreds of bikers roared northward on Atlantic Avenue, equal hundreds of students streamed southward.

Bike Week is a semi-annual bash in Daytona, attracting thousands of motorcycle enthusiasts.

Frankly, we preferred the bikers – not the drug-and-thug variety but mostly nice middleclass folks who simply love motorbikes. Each spring they haul the bike out of storage, polish it up, grow a beard (well, the guys do anyway) and head off to Daytona with their wives and girlfriends to roar around a bit, show off their hogs and admire other people's machines. There's black leather a-plenty but the height of chic seems to be bright yellow helmets matching bright yellow bikes. It's a happy, harmless weekend repeated in the fall before the Harley hibernates.

The problem wasn't the quality of the bikers, it was the quantity, in combination with a population explosion of students, already intoxicated with thoughts of the week ahead. Yeah, right!

Our two-hour, three-mile odyssey down Daytona's main drag was hell on wheels. But it gave us plenty of time to enjoy the passing scene – sleazy bars proffering all-day happy hours, grungy kiosks displaying grotesque T-shirts and baseball caps, dreary pizza joints, greasy hamburger joints and questionable motels of ancient vintage.

FLORIDA, EH? 55

Daytona Beach

Beyond the eastern wall of buildings, the broad Atlantic beach beckoned – wall-to-wall bodies of early bird arrivals, sharing the snowy sand with vehicles, predominantly SUVs and trucks. It's a Daytona tradition dating back decades, when car races were staged on the beach. We're all for maintaining traditions, but that's one we could do without.

So that's it for the carping and complaining. Fact is, we found much to enjoy in Daytona Beach. For Canadians, it's close, cheap and boasts 23 miles of beach. Best of all, a revitalization program is underway to reduce, reuse or recycle the sleaze. Several hotels are in place or under construction and others are undergoing renovation. (The downside of redevelopment is that accommodation prices may climb too high for most Canadians budgets.)

Bearded bikers are far less fierce than they appear.

Sunrise in Daytona Beach was glorious when all the human detritus had departed or collapsed somewhere out of sight. First peach, then pink, the eastern sky brightened, finally washing the fingernail of a moon out of the sky. The colour spread across the sea's slight turbulence before the red sun topped the horizon. On the beach, the tide had swept away most traces of the previous night's revelry, the gulls squabbled over a snack, formations of stately pelicans sailed low over the water seeking breakfast, early risers power-walked and children scavenged for shells. Daytona Beach was a good place to be.

Where to stay

This city is awash with hotels, motels, inns and b&bs. A handful of attractive and upscale lodgings is scattered along Atlantic Avenue, the beachfront street. But further afield, there are many more and with some exceptions, a block or two from the beach means better prices and quality. The Superior Small Lodgings program identifies smaller hotels, inspected annually for strict quality criteria. A booklet detailing 74 of these facilities is available free from Daytona Beach Area Convention and Visitors Bureau, 1-800-854-1234 or www.daytonalodging.com.

Nautilus Inn ☼ *($$)* ☼ *1515 S. Atlantic Ave., Daytona Beach 32118* ☼ *1-800-245-0560* ☼ *www.nautilus-inn.com*

Denure Tours, Lindsay, Ont. ☼ *1-800-668-6859* ☼ *www.denuretours.com*

Possibly the best beach-front deal in Daytona Beach is the Nautilus Inn, operated by the Canadian-owned motorcoach company, DeNure Tours of Lindsay, Ont. DeNure carries thousands of Canadians to Florida each winter. To catch as much sun as possible, they offer an Express Coach service, leaving Toronto (after pick-ups at various southern Ontario cities) at 9 a.m. and, with two drivers alternating, travelling all night to reach Daytona Beach at noon the following day. Frequent rest and meal stops, reclining seats and extra legroom, pillows, blankets and entertainment, make the trip more comfortable but at the end of the road, the Nautilus is no doubt a welcome sight.

DeNure's tours are particularly appealing to senior Canadians, so you'll see many silver crowns in the crowd, and amenities that cater to older travelers – sturdy grab bars in the bathrooms, shuffleboard in the garden, evening singsongs and lots of affordable and easy trips to shopping malls, restaurants and nearby attractions. But plenty of extended families and grandchildren, both independent travellers and coach tour participants, patronize the Nautilus.

Continental breakfast and afternoon social hour are included in the rate. Perks you won't find are mini-bars loaded with overpriced snacks, pricey bathrobes or bathroom toiletries. But you

Daytona Beach landmark is the historic clock tower, dating from 1936 and carefully preserved.

Daytona Beach makes Canadians welcome. The city's Canadian Sand Dollars program, which helps chop prices of hotels and attractions, restaurants and shops, is likely to extend into another year. It means 10 per cent off here, a free dessert there, two for one dinners. It all adds up. At **www.daytonabeach.com**, you'll find a 'just for Canadians' link that allows you to download Sand Dollar coupons. Or call 1-800-854-1234 for a free copy.

will find rooms that are immaculate, spacious and well equipped with balconies, TV, and, in efficiency suites, fully equipped kitchens. Downstairs, comfortable lounges invite conversation, games and socializing. The beach is just steps away and there's a heated swimming pool at the back door. And best of all, the friendly staff actually know where Canada is.

Ocean Walk Village ❂ *($$$)* ❂ *300 N. Atlantic Ave., Daytona Beach 32118* ❂ *1-877-845-WALK* ❂
www.oceanwalkvillage.com

This new kid on the block is setting a new standard for Daytona Beach, leading a revitalization drive that could have far-reaching consequences for the city. Ocean Walk Village is a $250 million oceanside development that occupies six square blocks of Atlantic shoreline and encompasses two resort hotels, vast meeting spaces, extensive entertainment facilities – and a chunk of beautiful beach, that's mercifully free of vehicular traffic. The landmark coquina clocktower and bandshell dating from 1936 have been preserved and hosts summer-long programs of free concerts, from country to jazz to Celtic to Spanish guitar.

The 746-room Adam's Mark Resort includes a five-acre Adventure Center with some new twists on getting wet – 12 water slides, for starters, including a three-level tree house with six slides. On the dry side, there are three nine-hole miniature golf courses, a two-level go-kart track and an arcade of more than 130 games. Six restaurants, a night-lit volleyball court, and an 18,000-sq.-ft. ballroom for entertaining a few of your closest friends round out the amenities.

Next door, the twin-towered Ocean Walk Resort doubles as both hotel and residence, with 176 condominium suites and 124 timeshares in each tower, all handsomely appointed with full kitchens, washer/dryers and Jacuzzis. An indoor golf training centre and an outdoor heated 'lazy river' pool, encircling an island putting green add to the fun.

Ocean Walk Shoppes comprise four levels of upscale boutiques plus a 10-screen movie theatre. Concerts, conferences, car shows and even rodeos will take place just across the street at Ocean Center, now part of the new development and set for major expansion.

Sights and Sounds

Ponce de Leon Lighthouse Museum ☻ 4931 S. Peninsula Dr., Ponce Inlet 32127 ☻ 386-761-1821 ☻ www.ponceinlet.org

Getting around

The complimentary VOTRAN beach tram operates on the beach from International Speedway to Seabreeze Blvd. during daylight hours.

A truly great lighthouse, this 175-foot National Historic Landmark, completed in 1887, has saved many a seaman's life on a stretch of shore that still strikes dread to sailors' hearts. And it's easy to see why. Major wrecks that have occurred here are recounted in graphic detail in the lighthouse museum. In 1565, seven ships of the French fleet were cast on the rocks by a big storm and their crews slaughtered by the Spaniards. In 1862, the USS Monitor sank

Besides the lighthouse, there's a superb museum of maritime artifacts and history.

in a storm off Cape Hatteras and its wreck was finally rediscovered in 1973. In 1897, the SS Commodore, a tugboat, went down. Its wreck was found in 1960. In 1945, the luxury liner, the Andrea Doria, with 1,706 crew and passengers aboard, collided with the Stockholm and rolled over. The chilling catalogue of horror goes on and on, tempered some-what by an absorbing history of lighthouses, from 180 BC in Egypt, when huge fires were lit in open lanterns, through the coal fires of the 1500s, the candles and oil lamps of the 1700s, the invention of the hollow-wick lamp in 1781 and finally in 1822 the fabulous Fresnel 'Lenticular Apparatus' which, thanks to its multiple facets, could focus 83 per cent of the light on the distant horizon. You can climb to the top of the lighthouse if you're so inclined or stay below to visit the site's other features – several keepers' cottages, a giftshop and the F.D. Russell, a 46-foot tugboat built in 1938. The lighthouse and museum are open daily except Christmas. Adults: $5: Children 11 and under: $1.50.

The beachfront bandshell at Daytona is just one venue in the exciting Florida International Festival, staged every second year.

Florida International Festival ✪ *Late July* ✪ *Various venues*
✪ *904-257-7790* ✪ *www.fif-lso.org*

Music fills the air when the Florida International Festival unveils a veritable feast of concerts, dance and comedy. This bi-annual event (2003, 2005, 2007) is headlined by the London Symphony Orchestra, which has made Daytona Beach its unofficial summer home for more than three decades. But that venerable institution, some 100 musicians strong, is joined by an eclectic line-up of talent. From Cape Breton's Natalie MacMaster to the Miami Steel and Percussion Group, from Bob Newhart to the Mystical Arts of Tibet, from traditional jazz to contemporary dance, Daytona Beach rocks for 17 rhythmic days. Top ticket price is about $65, but many concerts are free. There are mini concerts showcasing chamber groups, a 'New Horizons' series for newcomers, and special performances in shopping malls and business offices. A recent treat for moms-in-waiting and their unborn was 'Mothers-to-B Minor', a program based on the 'Mozart effect', a theory that links listening to Mozart with enhanced higher brain function.

Sport Fishing ✪ *Dozens of charter companies offering deep sea fishing expeditions have their headquarters along the waterfront just west of the Ponce de Leon Lighthouse. Your hotel can recommend the best and may even supply discount tickets.*

The Casements ✪ 25 Riverside Dr., Ormond Beach ✪ 386-676-3216

Now a community arts centre, this former home of John D. Rockefeller was abandoned for years. When it was finally rescued, the house was a mess beyond belief– smashed plaster and windows, leaking ceiling, broken woodwork. But today, it serves as a community resource centre with a delightful little recital hall with near-perfect acoustics and large dance studio. The high-ceilinged rooms and spacious garden are the setting for many community events from concerts to antique shows to boy scout activities. But the greatest drama of this place, aside from its priceless Steinway square grand piano, is the fact that it survived. To compare today's house with pre-restoration photographs is to appreciate the vision and determination of the city fathers and volunteer fund-raisers whose dedication made it happen.

Daytona Beach Events

Speed weeks – early February
Bike Week – early March
Spring Break – mid-March
Pepsi 400 – early July
Biketoberfest – mid-October

Sugar Mill Botanical Gardens ✪ 950 Old Sugar Mill Rd., Port Orange ✪ 386-767-1735

Way back in 1804 Patrick Dean of the Bahamas received a grant of 995 acres from the Spanish government and established a plantation. Sugar was produced here until 1836 when a fire destroyed most of the mill. Newly rebuilt, it was used to extract salt from sea water during the civil war and then abandoned. These days, some of the walls and the machinery have been restored but best of all is a pleasant 12-acre botanical garden maintained by the Volunteer Botanical Gardens of Volusa. Beneath towering shade trees interspersed with plenty of park benches, you'll find interesting plantings including a fern grotto and a butterfly garden. And for clock watchers, there's a human sundial that tells you the time of day if you stand on the current month. Open daily, dawn to dusk.

Daytona Flea and Farmers Market ✪ *Hwy. 92 at I-95* ✪ *Take VOTRAN bus from beachside hotels* ✪ *336-253-3330*
✪ *www.daytonafleamarket.com*

With some 1,000 vendors under one roof, selling both new and used merchandise, this is a market for shop-aholics. Open Fri-Sun, it offers free admission and free parking.

Good Eats ...

Inlet Harbor Marina and Restaurant ✪ *($$)* ✪ *133 Inlet Harbor Rd., Ponce Inlet 32127* ✪ *386-322-5501* ✪ *www.inletharbor.com*

Near the lighthouse and perched on the Intercoastal Waterway, this low rambling restaurant evokes the sea – in both menu and décor. If you wanna be . . . under the sea . . . this is the next best thing with its sea green and blue walls, its tables and even the bar stools decorated with fanciful fishes and flowers.

**Daytona Beach Convention and Visitors Bureau
1-800-854-1234 or www.daytonabeach.com.**

It's really two restaurants in one – inside and outside, with a kitchen for each. It's casual but good, open seven days a week for lunch and dinner and of course specializing in seafood. No reservations – it's first come, first served.

The Dancing Avocado Kitchen ✪ *($$)* ✪ *110 S. Beach St. Daytona Beach* ✪ *904-947-2022*

This funny, funky restaurant emphasizes healthy foods with special flare. Try an avocado melt (or a tuna or chicken one if avocado is not your favourite). Or the day's special – grilled or broiled 'today's catch' on a bun with lots of veggies. Prices are modest, wait staff is fun, the funky décor runs to black walls, multi-hued wooden chairs and signs like 'Beware Attack Gekko.'

Steve's Restaurant ✪ *($-$$)* ✪ *1620 S. Atlantic Ave.* ✪ *904-252-9444 and 1584 S. Nova Rd., Daytona Beach, 904-252-0101*

Big, busy and inexpensive, these old-style restaurants aren't fancy but they serve ample breakfasts, lunches and dinners, with most entrees under $10. The Greek-style bread, made on premises is excellent.

Sanford – From citrus to celery to chic

Sanford is a hidden jewel – a small town with an interesting history and a promising future, less than an hour's drive north-east of Orlando.

As 'progress' passed it by, Sanford fell asleep a few decades ago, thus preserving its small town charm and Victorian architecture.

Back when steamships plied the St. Johns River, carrying passengers and goods down from Jacksonville, and Henry Flagler's railway chugged south to the Keys, Sanford was a thriving port and commercial centre. But the steamships went to drydock; the railway rolled into the roundhouse. The celery crops that made Sanford the world's largest shipper of celery moved south to more fertile farmlands. Killer frosts and disease wiped out the citrus industry. Orlando's glitzy theme parks monopolized the travelling public. Sanford nodded off.

Now Sanford is enjoying a renaissance. After the 1887 fire, the town was rebuilt using sturdy brick. Today 23 buildings from that late 19th century period are listed on the National Register of Historic Places. Block after block of cobbled streets, lined with splendid old homes shaded by tall oaks, make this a walker's paradise. The downtown business district is lined with quaint shops and restaurants, all pressed tin ceilings and interesting antiques – there are 175 dealers in 20 shops, all within a two-block radius. The Helen Stains Theatre, in a renovated old movie house, provides live drama and musicals. There's a farmer's market, Oktoberfest and several other festivals year-round. In December, about a dozen historic homes open for holiday tours and in spring there's a garden tour.

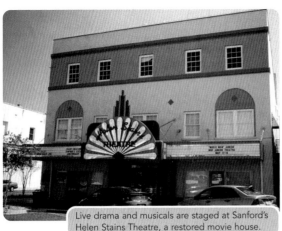

Live drama and musicals are staged at Sanford's Helen Stains Theatre, a restored movie house.

Terminus for **Amtrak's Auto Train**, the town also boasts the fourth largest international airport in Florida. That means a million or more arrivals each year – prosperity for Sanford but pressure on the town's merchants and services. Hurry on down before 'progress' takes its inevitable toll.

Sanford

A short walk from Sanford's Magnolia Square are antiques, historic houses, cobbled streets and lovely gardens.

Magnolia Square is the heart of the downtown historic district. A handsome clock tower presides over a charming cobbled parkette dotted with benches and flowers. From here you can stroll, admiring the antique stores, gift shops and pleasant restaurants.

Da Vinci ✪ *($$)* ✪ *107 Magnolia Ave., Sanford 32771* ✪ *407-323-1388* at the foot of Magnolia Square, occupies a splendid old building that once housed the Sanford Herald. Tall windows, high tin ceilings and chandeliers create a tony setting for an eclectic European-influenced menu with dinner entrees priced under $20. Salads, sandwiches and pastas provide affordable lunches. Open Tuesday to Saturday.

Morgan's Gourmet Café ✪ *($-$$)* ✪ *112 E. First St., Sanford 32771* ✪ *407-688-4745* is a long, narrow high-ceilinged restaurant serving lunch and dinner. Judging from the land-office lunch-time business we observed, the modest prices and enthusiastic unsolicited testimonial from a patron, this place is a local favourite. Open Monday to Saturday.

Ice cream and antiques – a tempting combination.

And how about combining ice cream and antiques. *Granny's on Magnolia Square* ✪ *201 E. First St., Sanford 32771* ✪ *407-322-7544* is a rambling collector's emporium with an ice cream bar near the back. And such ice cream! Retirees Joyce and Bernard Fitzgerald buy ice cream from a local company that prefers real ingredients over chemicals, producing a fabulous home-made taste. If your cholesterol can stand it, try 'Almond Joy', 'the only ice cream you can chew,' according to Bernard. Several of the 16 flavours are fat-free or low-fat. In summer, it could be peaches and cream. At St. Patrick's Day, it's green. Go ahead! Sample them all.

Down by the water . . .

The mighty **St. Johns River** which flows into **Lake Monroe** remains a fine asset for Sanford, providing a lengthy stretch of waterfront recreational facilities, walkways and beautiful vistas.

Otters Seafood Restaurant ❂
Hidden Harbor Marina, 4380 Carraway Pl., Sanford 32771

❂ *407-323-3991*

From Great Lakes troop carrier to luxurious cruise ship, the Romance docks at Sanford pier

Otters is a sprawling place with bargain-priced daily specials – all-you-can-eat dinners priced from $9 to $15. Housed in a former yacht club, the restaurant, as its name implies, specializes in seafood but for landlubbers, chicken and beef are also available. Open daily from 11 a.m. On weekends, there's live entertainment.

River Ship Romance ❂ *433 North Palmetto Ave. Sanford 32771*
❂ *1-800-423-7401* ❂ *407-321-5091* ❂ *www.rivershipromance.com*

A pleasant cruise and a bountiful banquet – that's Captain Bob Hopkins' formula for hospitality. And it seems to work. His handsomely appointed ship carries over 200 passengers per trip – plenty of Canadians among them – to view the countryside and enjoy dining and dancing. Its deep cool interior, all polished brass and dark red upholstery, is air conditioned. Outside you can choose a deck in sun or shade. A three-hour luncheon cruise costs $35.

Higgins House, first B&B in Sanford, also offers an outstanding garden, plus eco and heritage tours.

The Romance is a 98-foot former Great Lakes troop carrier, built in 1942. During wartime, she carried Canadian and American troops, patrolling the locks at **Sault Ste. Marie**. Later, the ship performed search and rescue missions – the sinking of the **Edmund Fitzgerald**, immortalized in **Gordon Lightfoot's** great song, was one of her calls. Purchased in 1995, the ship enjoyed a six-month refurbishment before emerging for cruise duty.

And so to bed and breakfast ...

Higgins House Bed & Breakfast ✪ (*$$*) ✪ *420 Oak Ave., Sanford 32771* ✪ *1-800-584-0014* ✪ *407-324-9238* ✪ *www.higginshouse.com*

The first bed and breakfast in Sanford – in fact in the county – **Higgins House** has been a 12-year labour of love for Roberta and Walt Padgett. Empty for two years before its rescue, it had already begun to succumb to Florida's twin plagues – weather and termites. The Padgetts have transformed it into a handsome and welcoming Victorian restoration, evoking its 1894 origins, with walls finished in deep rich colours, the heart oak floors gleaming, the rooms furnished with handsome antiques. A comfy little downstairs pub offers drinks and TV and a copious breakfast is served in the dining room.

The Padgetts – she's an OR nurse, he's a retired school teacher – are dynamite gardeners. Roberta's specialty is orchids while Walt, a Master Gardener, maintains a varied flower and vegetable garden for an enviable ten months of the year. The best views of the garden are perhaps from the outdoor hot tub.

Eco-adventure and heritage tours are offered by Higgins House. Three-to-five-day programs may encompass hiking and canoeing, birding, historical sites and buildings. They start at $295.

Higgins House welcomes Canadians with a 10 per cent discount on lodging for 'Florida, Eh?' readers who mention or show this book.

Agricultural Heritage

Demonstration Garden and Student Museum ✪ *301 W. Seventh St., Sanford 32771* ✪ *407-320-0520* ✪ *Open weekdays 1:30-4, free admission.*

Celery and citrus moved south but gardens and gardening are still major Sanford obsessions. And Walt Padgett is at the centre of the action.

Together with volunteer **Master Gardeners of Seminole County**, working with junior high school students, Walt has helped to develop an award-winning 10,000-square-foot **Demonstration Garden** that provides learning experiences for the entire community. Begun in 1998, the project demonstrates various plants and growing techniques – herbs, field crops such as corn and sugar cane, shade plants, a pioneer vegetable garden and an historic rose garden, a knot garden of vegetable greens, a butterfly garden and a tropical garden.

The gardens' mission, Walt explained, is 'to teach kids that food doesn't come out of cans.' Guided by Master Gardeners, the youngsters plant and harvest, and sometimes get to take home what they've grown. The public can visit the gardens and query Master Gardeners about

Master Gardeners of Seminole County maintain a huge demonstration garden where school groups and community learn about plants and planting.

gardening techniques and the viability of specific plants.

The **Demonstration Garden** occupies a once-fallow school playground. In a city park fronting the school, a fledgling **Historic Arboretum** is taking shape, each slender sapling carefully identified. For the future, a complete horticultural centre, including the arboretum and Master Gardener gardens, is envisioned.

Smack in the middle of all this gardening, a 1916 brick school, discarded for more modern facilities, has become a **Student Museum** where grade four students from across **Seminole County** share hands-on encounters with history.

At The Villages, retirement is a merry business, replete with hobbies, games and socializing.

After careful orientation in home classrooms, the kids are bussed to the museum where they participate in pioneer activities, all with agricultural themes. They may make butter or card and spin cotton grown in the Demonstration Garden.

Our favourite room was 'Grandma's Attic', a wondrous assortment of antique appliances like a roller wringer, treadle sewing machine, ice cream freezer, spinning wheel, loom, antique brass instruments and uniforms, an old phone and a wood-burning cook stove. The museum also displays a fascinating photographic record of the town's history.

Museum of Seminole History (300 Bush Blvd., Sanford 32773 ✪ 407-665-2489 ✪ Open Tues-Sat) traces the area's history with artifacts and exhibits. Admission is free.

Flea World ✪ Hwy. 17/92 between Sanford and Orlando ✪ www.fleaworld.com. Billing itself as the largest flea market in America, this teeming hub of second-hand commerce, open Fri., Sat. and Sun. 9-6, also includes a 200-store antique market.

Quiet Retirement? Not at The Villages

The Villages ✪ 1100 Main St., The Villages, 32159 ✪ 1-800 -245-1081
✪ www.thevillages.com

Okay, anyone for pickleball? (That's a net game played with vinegar-soaked cucumbers and a paddle). Seminars on new money scams and how to avoid them? Unlimited free golf? Karaoke? A performance of Madame Butterfly? Tennis, anyone? Water volleyball? Yoga? Line Dancing? Synchronized swimming? Astrology? Care to join the harmonica players, the acoustical string band, the cloggers?

Activities like these keep retirees hopping at **The Villages**, a remarkable self-contained development, 23 miles south of Ocala.

Founded in 1972, The Villages' adobe buildings and red tile roofs are reminiscent of a Spanish colonial town, with myriad amenities, security, round-the-clock recreation and wall-to-wall social life. The place has its own newspaper, TV and radio stations plus a dozen restaurants, churches, a hospital and medical centre, 12 miles of trails, fishing lakes, 12 heated swimming pools – all accessible by the Villages' preferred mode of transportation, the golf cart. This is a 55-plus community, but children and grandchildren are much in evidence.

There are over 15,000 homes and some 28,000 residents. Home prices start at about US$70,000, while some top the $400,000 mark. People who are serious about Florida retirement get a special inducement to check out The Villages. You can fly into Orlando Airport, to be chauffeured back to the check-in centre, then stay at one of the villas for up to seven nights. Rents start at US$150 for a three-night stay, but you get back $150 village dollars to spend in shops, restaurants, golf courses and other recreation facilities as you do your research.

Mount Dora's historic architecture adds to its picturesque ambience, appealing to walkers and shoppers.

Coffee, sweets and books nurture life's vital needs at Dickens.

Mount Dora – Quaint and then some

Mount Dora, a pretty town on Lake Dora, due south of Ocala National Forest, 25 miles north of Orlando, is already popular with Canadians. The Lake County Visitors Bureau says nearly half the town's foreign visitors are Canadian. What they find is a collection of upscale shops, all frills and fuss, souvenirs by the truckload, antiques and collectibles by the tonne, restaurants and tea rooms. It's a town made for walking but you can hop aboard a narrated trolley ride or a restored steam train for short jaunts.

The year-round festival roster presents music and literature in March, a sailing regatta in April, bicycles and crafts in October, antiques in November, January and February, and lots of Christmas events in December. With 14 lakes dotting the area, activities in and on the water abound.

Stores and Restaurants

Dickens-Reed Bookstore ✪ *140 W. Fifth Ave.* ✪ *352-735-5950* offers about 40,000 new and used books – including some by Canadian authors – plus gifts, greeting cards and an adjacent snack bar with deep couches and small tables for coffee and treats. Open seven days a week, the store sponsors author book signings, poetry readings and storytelling sessions for the tads.

If you're going all to the dogs, hurry over to *Piglet's Pantry* ✪ *400 North Donnelly Street* ✪ *1-888-Piglet4 or 352-735-9779* ✪ *www.pigletspantry.com*, a 'gourmet dog bakery' with a huge selection of treats and accessories for pampered pooches – and a few for our feline friends too. The store's namesake, Piglet, is a retired racing greyhound who, with trusted assistants, Tigger and Kricket, taste-tests every product. Or so he claims. He also testifies that products – such as Bow Wow Bon Bons, Piglet pizza or Kricket Krunchies – are all natural with no added salt, sugar or preservatives. The website offers mail order.

The Frosty Mug, ❂ *($-$$)* ❂ *411 N. Donnelly St.* ❂ *352-383-1696* ❂ *www.thefrostymug.com* downstairs in the Renaissance Building, is a fine old-fashioned pub – beamed ceiling, dark oak bar, stained glass and 50 varieties of good beer. Thora Einarsson, a vivacious blonde newcomer from Iceland, offers an all-round menu with some Scandinavian touches. Open daily except Mondays for lunch, dinner and Sunday brunch, with a happy hour plus live entertainment (classical guitar, folk or jazz).

At last . . . a decent cup of tea. In a proper china tea pot. *The Windsor Rose English Tea Room and Restaurant* ❂ *144 West 4th Ave.* ❂ *352-735-2551* gets it right, seven days a week, with high tea, (served all day), afternoon tea, lunches and dinners. The lengthy high tea menu includes steak and mushroom pie, Cornish pasty, Scotch egg and sandwiches. For afternoon teas, save space for the usual finger sandwiches, scones with clotted cream and jam, and pastries. The amusing menu offers a short course in English vernacular – the true meaning of bonnet and boot (the hood and trunk of a car) or vest (an undershirt.) English groceries are for sale.

Restored steam train takes visitors for a ride at Mount Dora, a quaint village north of Orlando.

Lodgings

The Lakeside Inn
❂ *($$$-$$$$)*
❂ *100 North Alexander St.* ❂ *1-800-556-5016* ❂ *www.lakeside-inn.com*

The Lakeside Inn is a vintage hotel, just steps from Mount Dora's downtown. When we visited, the Canadian maple leaf flew outside, alongside flags from Britain, Germany and Australia, honouring current guests. A deep verandah rims the building, providing a fine view of Lake Dora. Inside, there's live jazz in the lounge on weekends, and the **Beauclaire Restaurant** serves a Sunday champagne brunch plus varied breakfast, lunch and dinner offerings ($$$). The 88 guest rooms include suites, garden parlours and lakefront rooms. Guests are pampered with plenty of extras – there's a pool and pool bar, boat slips, tennis-courts and golf, a guests-only beach with chairs and a continental breakfast buffet included in the rate.

Emerald Hill Inn ✪ *27751 Lake Jem Road, Mount Dora 32757* ✪ *($$-$$$)* ✪ *1-800-366-9387* ✪ *www.emeraldhill.net*

Our favourite part of Mount Dora wasn't in Mount Dora at all. It was the **Emerald Hill Inn**, a lovely old plantation house overlooking Lake Victoria, five miles (8 km) from Mount Dora (15 if you get lost as we did), and 25 miles north of Orlando.

We approached Emerald Hill just at sunset, driving down a leafy corridor amid the intoxicating scent of orange blossoms.

A proper cuppa along with British specialties are offered at the Windsor Rose English Tea Room.

We were ushered swiftly through the big deep house to the gardens overlooking the lake and a sunset to remember – the sky awash in pinks and purples, mirrored in the lake's still waters. When the glory faded, we strolled back up to the house through azaleas, camellias and magnolia bushes, dwarfed by towering pines and live oaks draped with moss.

In one corner of the garden, park benches encircle a massive fireplace – the setting for weddings and special events. As a registered notary, our hostess, Colleen McGinley, can perform wedding ceremonies and frequently does. She can co-ordinate the entire event, including a reception and gourmet treats in her huge screened Florida room.

Colleen and her husband, Ron Oimoen, have been innkeepers for only a couple of years but they have the hang of it. Self-professed computer nerds, (here's one place where Internet connectivity wasn't a problem), they're escapees from California's silicone society. Their 5,000-sq.-ft. limestone house, with four guestrooms, was built for a citrus grower in 1941. The living room, with a huge coquina rock fireplace, a cathedral ceiling, and deep couches, leads to the airy Florida room, overlooking the garden and the lake.

Breakfast in the Florida room is tasty, ample and enhanced by the view of the garden and lake and the sound of singing birds. The house specialty is fritters – apples or pineapple – but the menu may run to poached eggs and smoked salmon or potato pancakes with plum chutney. By special request, Colleen may prepare a picnic lunch or candle light dinner for her guests.

Visitors can rent kayaks, canoes or paddle boats, as well as bicycles nearby. There's a dock at the foot of the garden and fishing on the lake.

Canada's red maple leaf joins flags of other visitors' nations at the venerable Lakeside Inn, overlooking Lake Dora.

Traditional European breads and this-minute pizzas are among Yalaha Bakery specialties.

Phone numbers

Although many Florida inns advertise toll-free numbers, very few extend that courtesy to Canadians. As well, the state's telephone area codes are changing. We've done our best to provide current numbers, but these two factors may result in calls that can't be completed. Do remind innkeepers that Canadians comprise a huge market in Florida and the courtesy of a toll-free number is simply good business.

Yalaha Bakery ✪ *8210 County Road 48, Yalaha.* ✪ *352-324-3779*
✪ *www.yalahabakery.com*

Head west from Emerald Hill to Yalaha on County Road 48 and out in the middle of nowhere you'll find a gem of a bakery/café, where a German baker makes the healthy breads of his homeland. The building is eye-catching. Its colourful Bavarian-style mural suggests the style of the products within – wholesome, hearty, organic breads and buns, including sour doughs and whole grains, German rye and Kalamata olive loaves, French raisin and walnut – and a whole lot more, all topped off by decadent strudels and tortes and in December, Christstollen, Germany's historic Christmas cake. Inside, you can order substantial sandwiches (under $5). Outside on the patio, a big pizza oven delivers unique pizzas, made to order, and served at umbrella tables overlooking orange groves. Each Saturday, local musicians and artists come to entertain. Open Mon.-Sat. 8-5.

Fort Lauderdale – Another Venice

Fort Lauderdale calls itself **'the Venice of America'**, which probably startles the four **real** Venices – in California, Louisiana, Illinois, and of course, Florida's west coast. Never mind. What they mean is that they have canals – lots of them. Fort Lauderdale is laced with 165 miles of waterways, buzzing with 40,000 resident yachts. Water taxis ply the waterways, linking hotels, restaurants and night spots. Several riverfront cruise companies offer dinner cruises or daytime guided voyages through the canals. We even spied Theodore II, escaping the Halifax winter for Fort Lauderdale's New River.

More than half a million Canadians visit Fort Lauderdale each year, attracted by an affluent, dynamic city, blessed with temperate weather and sunshine a-plenty, to say nothing of **Broward County's** 23 miles of ocean-front beaches. Dining, nightlife, shopping, sports, theatre, music and historic sites mean there's something for everyone.

The hot spot for seeing and being seen, for fine dining and entertainment is Las Olas Boulevard.

The city is notably gay-friendly and the rainbow flag flies at many establishments. The area boasts more than 100 gay-owned hotels, bars and restaurants and the second largest Metropolitan Community Church congregation in the U.S. **The Rainbow Carpet Guide and Map**, free from the Visitors Bureau, provides listings.

The arts scene is lively. The **Riverwalk** arts and entertainment district includes the splendid **Broward Center for the Performing Arts, the Museum of Discovery and Science with its IMAX theatre, the Florida Grand Opera, Old Fort Lauderdale, Museum of Art, the Fort Lauderdale Film Festival**, and historic **Stranahan House**, all within walking distance of one another.

Canadians, including our favourite tugboat, Theodore, are welcome in Fort Lauderdale.

Fort Lauderdale

Underwater it's also busy. A natural reef system, accessible from numerous beaches, is augmented by some 80 artificial reefs, some of them developed by sinking everything from a 435-foot freighter to a 94-foot DC-4 aircraft to an oil rig.

May is **Scuba Month**, anchored on the third weekend by the three-day **OceanFest**.

Thousands of divers and snorkellers convene for contests, demonstrations and a dive trade show plus both shore and boat dives during which music is piped underwater for their entertainment. The event prompts many special hotel and dive packages. *OceanFest* ✪ *1-800-327-8150* ✪ *www.oceanfest.com*

To promote its underwater activities, the region offers a 20-minute scuba diving video, **The Wrecks and Reefs of Greater Fort Lauderdale**, available free from the Visitors Bureau (1-800-22-SUNNY).

Fine musical sculpture accents entrance to the Broward Center for the Performing Arts.

Places to see

Stranahan House ✪ *335 SE 6th Ave., Fort Lauderdale 33301* ✪ *954-524-4736* ✪ *www.stranahanhouse.com*

Fort Lauderdale's 100-year history, from isolated trading post to chic tourist mecca, is encapsulated within a single building – Stranahan House, Broward County's oldest building.

Frank Stranahan came to Fort Lauderdale from the Ohio coal mines and stayed to build an empire. His house began as a trading post, purveying beads and fabric, guns and ammunition, canned goods, (especially peaches) and coveted sewing machines to Seminole Indians while relieving them of alligator hides, exotic feathers, fish and game to send north.

But it was his young wife, Ivy, whose forward-thinking ideas made such a lasting impact on the area and earned her the loving Seminole title of 'little white mother'. Until her death in 1971, Ivy Stranahan pushed to provide education and employment options for the Seminoles, and ultimately persuade local politicians to allocate reservation land for them.

Stranahan House was Fort Lauderdale's first trading post, later a family home that's now a museum.

The three-story house (two stories open to visitors) contains some original furniture, augmented by carefully selected pieces of the 1913-15 period when it was the Stranahans' home.

A realistic mannequin of Ivy occupies an upstairs parlour but her brilliant presence, contrasted against her husband's morose but moral persona, imbues the house, where dedicated docents, led by Linda Fox, invoke their memories. Tours are offered Wed.-Sun. Adm: adults $5, children $2.

CanadaFest is a big free fun beach party in nearby Hollywood. Usually the first weekend of February, it attracts up to 225,000 visitors over three days. Originally a fete for French-Canadians, who predominate in that area, it's attracting English-speakers too, both Canadian and American. Canadian performers strut their stuff in both languages and exhibitors promote goods and services such as travel insurance and accommodations.

This non-profit festival is organized by Yves Beauchamp, a long-time escapee from Canadian winters, who is now publisher of the French-language Canadian newspaper, **Le Soleil de la Floride** (2117 Hollywood Blvd., Hollywood 33020 ☻ 954-922-1800 ☻ www.lesoleildelafloride.com or www.canadafest.com)

National Car Rental Center ✪ *2555 Panther Pkwy., Sunrise, FL.*
✪ *954-835-8000* ✪ *www.nationl-ctr.com*

This all-purpose sports and entertainment complex is close to Sawgrass Mills, 10 miles west of town. It's the home of the Florida Panthers hockey team but, like Toronto's old Maple Leaf Gardens, it serves also as a concert venue – Celine Dion, The Rolling Stones and Eminem were among recent luminaries singing to its cavernous interior. Tickets are available through TicketMaster (954-523-3309)

Nature up close

Thousands of sea turtles come ashore to lay their eggs from May to mid-September. These endangered animals can weigh up to 1,300 pounds and measure seven feet in length. Local conservationists find and excavate the nests, moving them to hatcheries for safekeeping, until the hatchlings can safely make their way into the ocean.

The **Anne Kolb Nature Center at Westlake Park,** a 1500-acre mangrove estuary and wildlife site, has hatchling release programs on Hollywood's North Beach. *(July-Sept.* ✪ *954-926-2410)* The **John U. Lloyd Beach State Park** (954-924-3859) and the **Museum of Discovery and Science** *(June-July* ✪ *954-713-0930)* feature summer turtle programs. A guide scouts out sea turtles preparing their nests and allows visitors to view the spectacle from a safe distance.

The legendary **Florida Everglades** are at Fort Lauderdale's western door and myriad tours and safaris are available from the city or from **Big Cypress** , the Seminole reservation north of the Everglades Parkway (Alligator Alley.) The **Ah-Tah-Thi-Ki Museum**, a fine overview of Seminole history, is nearby. (See '**Everglades**' chapter for details.)

For Shop-aholics

Fort Lauderdale's **Swap Shop** (954-791-7927) claims to be the largest indoor/outdoor flea market in the U.S. with 2,000 vendors spread over 80 acres. It's open seven days a week. There's a shuttle service from downtown hotels, free circus shows daily and live entertainment. The **Festival Flea Market Mall** in Pompano (954-979-4555) boasts over 850 stores, a video arcade, food court and an indoor farmer's market.

Seminole Tribe history is detailed at the Ah-Tah-Thi-Ki Museum near Fort Lauderdale, where the Everglades begin.

Sawgrass Mills Mall, 12801 West Sunrise Blvd., Sunrise, FL 33323 ✪ (10 mi. west of Fort Lauderdale) ✪ 954-846-2300 ✪ Open 7 days a week.

This vast sprawling complex requires plenty of stamina, loads of loot and sturdy shoes. It's said to be the largest discount and entertainment mall in the state, the country or the world, depending upon which promoter you encounter. Anyway it's big – really big, with 400 outlet stores, including major players in American retailing. Some 30 eateries populate the mall's Oasis.

Places to stay

For Lauderdale accommodations are on the pricey side, but deals do exist. Many hotels offer discount carrots for Canadians – 'stay two weeks and get a third week in Canadian dollars' was popular recently. One hotel accepted loonies at par for a 12-week stay while others simply offered discounts. The **Superior Small Lodging** program sets standards for dozens of quality properties under 50 rooms. A directory is available from the Visitors Bureau.

Hampton Inn ✪ ($$) ✪ 250 N. Andrews Ave., Fort Lauderdale FL 33301 ✪ 954-924-2700 ✪ www.hamptoninnftlauderdale.com

New hotels are springing up like mushrooms in Fort Lauderdale. A recent arrival is a **Hampton Inn** in the centre of the city, a comfortable 156-room hotel. Breakfast is included – the usual boring little boxes of

Fort Lauderdale's pleasant Riverwalk leads to the flowery gardens of the Broward Center.

cereal, commercial bagels with cream cheese and fruit. But elevating it above the ordinary is a basket of warm biscuits besides a crock pot of fresh hot sausage gravy, the personal touch of food service manager Loretta Jackson, who starts her day at 5 a.m. to prepare this delicious southern treat.

Though the hotel is equipped with all the technological perks that business travellers like – a business centre with high-speed Internet access and copying machines, meeting rooms and fitness facilities – there's a swimming pool and guest laundry, refrigerators and microwaves in each room, and it's walking distance from downtown.

Crowne Plaza Sawgrass Mills ✪ 13400 W. Sunrise Blvd., Sunrise FL 33323 ✪ 954-851-1020 ✪ www.crowneplaza.com.

Also new and upscale, the **Crowne Plaza Sawgrass Mills** serves business travellers but, located close to the **Sawgrass Mills Mall** and the huge **National Car Rental** entertainment and sports complex, it may appeal to shoppers and star-gazers too. Celine Dion was among stars recently spotted in the hotel lobby. The hotel offers a value package for patrons of the entertainment complex – a room and breakfast for two, transportation to the event and overnight parking for about $125. Guests must present their concert or game ticket at check-in to qualify.

The hotel's 250 rooms each contain refrigerator and microwave, a two-line phone with data port and even an ironing board and iron. A fitness room, heated pool, restaurant and business centre take care of other needs. Staff speak Dutch, English, Italian, Portuguese, Spanish – and Canadian. The sales manager is multi-lingual Wanita Charron, recently recruited from the Laurentians, north of Montreal.

Greater Fort Lauderdale Convention & Visitors Bureau
1-800-22-SUNNY or www.sunny.org

Bal Harbour – the Gold Coast's golden plaza

Bal Harbour Village ❂ 9700 Collins Ave., Bal Harbour, FL 33154 ❂ Hwy A1A north of Miami ❂ 305-866-0211 ❂ www.balharbourshops.com

If you're a shop-til-you-drop traveller, you're in good company. Surveys indicate that shopping is tops on many travellers' interest lists. And where better to pursue your hobby than an upscale shopping centre lined with 100 or more top name shops of Fifth Avenue descent, plus eateries that range from chic cafes to fine dining. And even some Canadian connections.

Welcome to **Bal Harbour Shops** on Florida's 'Gold Coast', perhaps named equally for its sun-drenched sand and its credit cards. Names like Armani, Dior and Chanel, Neiman Marcus and Saks Fifth Avenue set the tone, amid an open-air fantasy of water gardens, vivid koi, fountains, flowers and original art.

Water accents and sculpture make Bal Harbour Village a shopping centre like no other.

And Canadian connections? If you can't last another minute without maple syrup, drop by **Cookworks** where the genuine article from Paul Boivin of Abercorn, Que., joins some 50,000 other rare foods, herbs and oils, glassware, dishes, cutlery, the biggest assortment of pepper grinders ever assembled on one shelf unit and a tempting selection of cookbooks (including "How to Cook for Your Dog").

And there's more – you don't just buy the stuff, you learn how to use it. Cookworks sponsors twice-yearly cooking schools, ($75-$100 per session), inviting outstanding chefs and authors to share their expertise, in the store's own working kitchen.

Lush gardens, appealing swimming pools and the sea – that's the ravishing view from the balcony at the Sheraton Bal Harbour Resort.

A few steps more bring you to **Bal Harbour Gallery** and the ecstatic bronze dancers of ex-Montreal sculptor Esther Westheimer, keeping elegant company with Picasso, Matisse, Miro, Chagall and even Rembrandt. Co-owner Vivian Lacorra explains that the gallery, which has been here for nearly 12 years, selects artworks from outstanding artists worldwide – and ships customers' selections to any address in the world, fully insured.

And the mall food? No greasy spoons here. The **Bal Harbour Bistro** serves cappuccinos fit for Queen Street. And at **Carpaccio**, a bustling Italian restaurant, patrons wait patiently in line, confident that great food at affordable prices is worth waiting for. Carpaccio seats patrons both inside and out, within earshot of fountains and three-story water walls that fill the air with sounds of running water. Which is good, because the sound of running waiters can just about drown out the water. We've never seen waiters move so fast, serve so efficiently and still keep their good humour. The menu features Northern Italian delights such as white bean soup, interesting pastas and pizzas (lots of vegetarian possibilities there), seven variations on the veal theme, beef, chicken and succulent fresh seafood. And tiramisu, light as a feather, presented on a blue-bordered plate with chocolate swirls. Paradise enow!

Sheraton Bal Harbour Beach Resort ✪ *($$-$$$)* ✪ *9701 Collins Ave., Bal Harbour* ✪ *305-865-7511* ✪ *www.starwood.com/sheraton*

Completing the Bal Harbour story, the **Sheraton Bal Harbour Beach Resort** just across the street offers all the perks and treats that we've come to expect of this quality worldwide chain, from the sweeping lobby to the spacious rooms with their oversize dressing rooms, to the lush tropical gardens that separate the hotel from the oceanfront. A huge undulating swimming pool is rimmed by jolly yellow cabanas, each fitted with a TV set for those who just can't quit.

The hotel's spa, next to a well equipped fitness room, was another treat. Mayra and Elaine took us firmly in hand – literally – with aromatherapy treatments that untied the knots of weeks on the road and green tea facials that erased years from our faces – only temporarily, unfortunately.

Within the hotel, the **al Carbon Restaurant**, deep and dark, specializes in sizzling dinners, straight from the grill. Breakfast at the **Beach House** was Sheraton's usual lavish hot and cold buffet enhanced by a fine view of the ocean. Now that airlines are feeding their bottom lines by starving their passengers, the Sheraton has come to the rescue with '**meals-to-go**' – gourmet sandwiches, an antipasto plate, or tropical fruit plate, priced at $9.95, ($6.95 for kids) and far tastier than a bag of stale goldfish biscuits.

Miami and the Beaches – Diversity and then some

Miami is a young, brash, nouveau-riche city, constantly changing, beset by all the problems that growth and diversity can bring, endowed with all the bells and whistles that money can buy.

Luxurious hotels by the dozens, fabulous cuisine, dazzling nightlife, and outstanding museums and cultural centres are just the start.

You'll find cultural diversity that makes even Toronto's ethnic mix seem tame – nearly half the population is Spanish-speaking and it's not unusual to hear Portuguese, French, Creole, Italian, Patois, Yiddish, Russian, German, Dutch or Hebrew. Each group contributes its cultural heritage, festivals, food and music to the throbbing life of Miami. And with balmy weather averaging 75 deg. F. (23 C) plus miles of fine sand beaches, it's easy to enjoy.

Miami has paid a high price for fame. Movies and TV have painted lurid

One of Miami Beach's finest and tallest buildings is Old City Hall, built in 1920.

pictures of crime and depravity, and recent media coverage has emphasized problems generated by the city's divergent racial groups, poverty, drugs and Mafia-dominated past. It's hard to forget that Al Capone was once one of Miami's most frequent visitors.

But that was then. Fact is, Miami has taken aggressive action to root out crime and increase security. A special task force of undercover officers targets street criminals while another group points tourists toward their destinations. Police officers patrol the beach areas on foot or bike – even small all-terrain vehicles – and a squad known as the **Tourist Oriented Police** (TOP) works the airport and adjacent car rental areas. Miami was one of the first cities to regulate car rentals, requiring rental companies to provide maps and safety information and eliminating license plates that identified a car as a rental. The result has been a dramatic drop in crimes against tourists – 93 per cent over the past decade.

None of this means you can leave your car unlocked or drop your camera on the beach and expect to find it later. Sensible security precautions are a tourist's responsibility anywhere in the world, especially in a crowded international city.

South Beach – the Art Deco story

Nowhere is Miami's youth and vitality more evident than in **South Beach**, 'a place that knows no misfits'. Truly anything goes in this oceanfront community where seeing and being seen can be a full-time occupation and international celebrities rub shoulders with penny-pinching backpackers.

Ocean Drive faces the beach, lined on the west side by wall-to-wall restaurants and clubs, each with its sound system cranked up a bit higher than its neighbour's. The sidewalks are crowded with walkers and skate boarders, dodging the tables of al fresco diners. The street is full of cars, which seem to sit forever, inspecting one another's bumpers. The decibels are high, the energy is high, some of the people are high . . . it's round-the-clock party time.

Miami in general and South Beach in particular are especially friendly places for gay and lesbian travellers and several hotels and clubs cater specifically to this group. The Miami Convention and Visitors Bureau has issued **'Gay and Lesbian Miami'**, but for the latest on hotels, restaurants, and entertainment, visit www.GoGayMiami.com.

Miami Design Preservation League ✪ *1001 Ocean Drive, Miami Beach Miami Beach* ✪ *305-672-2014* ✪ *www.mdpl.org* ✪ *Open 10-4, daily.*

It's the architecture, however, that sets South Beach apart. The Art Deco district, now listed on the National Register of Historic Places, covers about a square mile – over 800 buildings – built in the distinctive style of the 1930s. Art Déco was a new idea for its time – streamlined, machine-inspired, with rounded corners, 'eyebrows' accenting windows, pastel colours and lots of modern materials such as glass block, neon lighting and chrome. Cheaply built during Depression years, probably funded by bootlegging and drug money, the buildings faced almost certain demolition until a group of Miami residents undertook a campaign of salvation and public education. Today, the buildings are carefully protected and restoration is rigidly controlled, right down to the exterior colours.

During mid-January, the **Miami Design Preservation League (MDPL)**, the area's watchdog and public educator, hosts **Art Deco Weekend** which began as a one-day event in 1976 and now attracts more than a quarter million visitors a year. The lengthy program ranges from thoughtful retrospectives on the

Tall palms and even taller skyscrapers frame a glowing sunset sky in Miami Beach, headquarters for round-the-clock fun.

Domino Park gets its name from non-stop games of dominos, punctuated by card games and local gossip.

history of the area to lively jazz concerts and beach parties.

Year-round, the League provides excellent tours – self-guided audio tours at $10 per person, Saturday morning 90-minute walking tours conducted by local historians and architects at $15 per person and guided bike tours at $15 (plus $15 for bike or rollerblade rental.) Another intriguing offering is the **Art Deco Underworld Tour** which explores Prohibition Days in Miami Beach, and investigates rooftop gambling and Al Capone's hangouts. It's offered a few times a year – check with MDPL for times and prices.

More to see

Ancient Spanish Monaster ✪, *16711 West Dixie Hwy., North Miami Beach, FL 33160* ✪ *305- 945-1461* ✪ *www.spanishmonastery.com*

When William Randolph Hearst wanted something, money was no object. Thus a 12th century Cistercian monastery from Segovia, Spain now resides in Miami. It seems that Hearst wanted the building for his fabled '**Xanadu**' in California. After he paid $500,000 for it in 1925, it was dismantled and shipped to New York. But fired up by a foot and mouth disease scare, customs officials insisted on opening all 11,000 crates, removing the stones and burning the hay in which they were packed. The result was chaos – they couldn't figure out which stones belonged in which crates. Hearst abandoned the project and the stones languished in a warehouse for 25 years before wealthy developers reassembled them – with some left over – at a cost of $1.5 million. Today it's open for visits and a popular place for weddings.

Vizcaya Museum & Gardens ✪ *3251 S. Miami Ave. Miami, FL* ✪ *305-250-9133* ✪ *www.vizcayamuseum.org*

The winter home of International Harvester executive James Deering, this 70-room Italian Renaissance mansion on Biscayne Bay, furnished with European antiques and surrounded by 10 acres of formal gardens, resembles a typical Italian villa. Built in 1916, its construction employed more than 1,000 workers – nearly 10 per cent of Miami's population at the time. Now a National Historic Landmark, Vizcaya hosts an annual Italian Renaissance Festival in March with comedy, arts, music, drama and food. Open daily except Christmas. Adm: adults $10, children 6-12 $5. Moonlight garden and general tours available.

The Wolfsonian-Florida International University ✪ *1001 Washington Ave., Miami Beach, FL 33139* ✪ *305-535-2622* ✪ *www.wolfsonian.org*

Handy to the Art Deco district in South Beach, The Wolfsonian is described as a museum of design and propaganda arts from the period 1885-1945. It's a packrat's heaven – chock full of furniture and artifacts, glass and ceramics, rare books, paintings, textiles, and a comprehensive collection of political propaganda from all across Europe and the U.S. The intent is to explore the way design has both altered and been altered by cultural changes, industrial innovation and persuasion. But it's also a fascinating overview of what modern civilization hath wrought.

Newport Pier, stretching into the ocean near Newport Beachside Resort, is a leisure oasis for all ages.

Neighbourhoods

Each of Miami's neighbourhoods has its own distinct personality, with local accents such as festivals or restaurants to match. **Coral Gables**

A Miami Beach institution since the early 1900s, Joe's Stone Crab Restaurant is famed for both seafood and key lime pie.

began life in the 1920s as utopia and remains a beautiful community of tall trees shading red-tiled Mediterranean style homes, now much sought after by the glitterati. **Coconut Grove Village** also dates from the twenties, though one section of town was built by émigrés from the Bahamas before the turn of the century. A hippie hangout in the sixties, the village is now moderately upscale and respectable. **Little Havana** and **Little Haiti** are home to vibrant Latino communities.

Where to stay

The list of hotels, motels, inns and hostels in the Greater Miami area would fill a substantial book. Our two samples are both in South Beach, but you'll find the whole glittering galaxy at the Miami Visitors Bureau website – www.tropicoolmiami.com.

Ocean Five Hotel and Bistro ✪ *($$$)* ✪ *436 Ocean Dr., Miami Beach 33139* ✪ *305-532-7093* ✪ *www.OceanFive.com*

Many buildings in the Art Deco district began life as not-too-pricey lodgings for northern visitors and have been reincarnated as chic boutique hotels. They now range from luxury to modest, from pricey oceanfront to more affordable back streets. Our choice was Ocean Five Hotel and Bistro, near the south end of town, walking distance from the lively round-the-clock party atmosphere, but mercifully out of earshot of the ghetto blasters and car horns. English, French, German and Spanish are spoken at the front desk.

This family-owned business incorporates a 56-room hotel and a next-door restaurant, as well as a deli-market just up the street. There's valet parking next to the hotel – a rare convenience in this congested area.

Renovated in 2001, the hotel reflects its Art Deco origins, with a creamy pastel exterior accented by dramatic vertical colour bars. Inside, the mood becomes Mediterranean/Mexican inspired by heavy wooden shutters, wooden furniture with wrought iron detail, marble bathrooms and earth-tone décor. There's free Internet access in the lobby and a small conference room for meetings.

Next door, the Bistro's façade is a fantasy of vines and flowers, with small tables for al fesco dining. Serving breakfast, lunch and dinner, the restaurant is dominated by a massive wood-burning pizza oven, though dinner menus extend beyond pizza to home-made pastas, seafoods and filet mignon, good salads and a dessert list headed up by tiramisu.

The Clay Hotel and Hostel ✪ *($)* ✪ *1438 Washington Ave., South Beach 33139* ✪ *1-800-379-CLAY* ✪ *www.clayhotel.com*

This budget-priced duo of lodgings claims a colourful past – it's said to be one of Al Capone's popular hangouts in the 1920s. In the 30s, Desi Arnaz started the rumba craze, more recently Sylvester Stallone, John Travolta and Sharon Stone made movies and Miami Vice filmed 10 episodes, all in this unique setting. Yet both hotel and hostel, the latter affiliated with International Hostelling, offer rock-bottom prices plus myriad amenities, such as 24-hour security, air conditioning, TV and guest kitchen and laundry, all just two blocks from the beach. Hotel rooms for

Greater Miami Convention & Visitors Bureau, 701 Brickell Ave., Suite 2700 Miami, FL 33131 ✪ **1-800-933-8448** ✪ **www.tropicoolmiami.com**

two start at under $50; hostel dorm rates are less than $20 while singles and doubles with private baths are also available. Built in 1925, the Clay is actually nine interlinked buildings, which include 17,000 sq. ft. of retail – six restaurants, an ice cream shop, others for gifts and bathing suits. There's even a house artist - Cuban expatriot Pedro Amador spends four days a week painting colourful tropical murals on the walls of the myriad corridors that connect the buildings.

Miami moves to a salsa beat

Think of **Miami** and you think of palm-lined streets of grand houses, the elegant opulence of **Coral Gables**, the moneyed ambience of **Miami Beach**.

But my Miami is different.

My Miami is **Little Havana**, a vibrant chunk of Cuba transported to Florida. My Miami moves to the beat of salsa. My Miami is great Latino food, smiling Latino hospitality and fun from dusk to dawn.

Little Havana hasn't always fared well at the hands of the media. Yet the best fun to be found in Miami happens in

Anyone can salsa but serious dancers adjourn to Starfish for lessons in the most complicated steps.

this community of Cuban exiles where the aroma of café Cubano and the beat of Cuban music fill the air. And despite Miami's high-priced cachet, Little Havana's food, fun, drinks and dancing are all affordable.

Calle Ocho, (Eighth Street), the main drag, is alive with Cuban influences – cigar shops where stogies are hand-rolled before your eyes, Domino Park where elderly gentlemen pass their days slapping down dominos, playing cards and gossiping.

But to get really fired up for Little Havana, I visited **Starfish** (1427 West Ave., Miami Beach ✪ 305-854-1606) for a lesson in the challenging art of salsa. Expatriate Cuban Omar Caraballo directs this happening place where you can take dance lessons each evening from Monday to Thursday, then return on weekends to practice your salsa steps in a happy party atmosphere that lasts until dawn. Salsa is an extremely physical dance with complicated footwork and body movement. Advanced dancers often perform in groups – anywhere from eight to 30 people – spinning, dipping, whirling, entwining, to the infectious Latino beat of singers, guitars, klaves and congos.

But don't be intimidated by the experts. With a few basic salsa steps, you'll be ready, as I was, to dance the night away.

Back in Little Havana, it's time for an authentic Cuban meal. One of the hottest spots is **La Esquina de Tejas** *(101 SW 12th Ave., Miami* ✪ *305/545-0337)* an unpretentious little eatery that attracts big name guests such as Madonna and Bill Murray. Ronald Reagen paid a visit in 1983. In fact his autograph is reproduced on the bilingual menu where a popular dish is rice and beans in a dozen or so incarnations – 'moros y cristianos' (moors and christians), referring to white rice and black beans. Another favourite is yuca al moho – mealy casava, fried, and drenched in a delicious vinaigrette and garlic sauce. My favourite was vaca frita – grilled shredded flank steak, marinated in herbs. Most main courses are under $10.

A famed Cuban singer, Wilfredo Meni, once dubbed 'the golden voice of Cuba' before his arrival in the U.S. 15 years ago, serenades dinner guests here with time-honored Cuban love songs.

In recent years, many other Latino groups have settled in Miami. A few blocks north of Little Havana is Little Haiti with its Creole flavours and Caribbean Marketplace, a reproduction of the famed Iron Market in Port-au-Prince.

A tropical paradise that prepares you for a long night of salsa, this palm-shaded stretch of sand. typical of Miami Beach, is part of the Newport Beachside Resort.

Further south, in South Beach, you'll encounter Casa Salsa, a Puerto Rican restaurant where a table is permanently reserved for singer Ricky Martin, a silent partner in the establishment. **Casa Salsa** *(524 Ocean Dr.* ☎ *305-604-5959)* is modest in size and appearance but the food is awesome – chicken breast stuffed with almonds and mango, banana leaf baked mahi topped with mango curried sauce, succulent lobster, shrimp and other seafood. Main course prices range from $17 to $29.

Infectious Latin beat resonates in Miami's Cuban quarter. At famed la Esquina de Tehas where Wilfredo entertains.

One more Miami landmark is worthy of note – The Newport Pier, heaven for die-hard fishermen of all ethnic origins. It's in Sunny Isles, part of Newport Beachside Resort. The Pier is free to guests at the Resort, $3 a day to others. Equipped with icey coolers, drinks and lunch, fishermen spend the day here, and rarely leave without a noteworthy catch. Best of all, they're a friendly bunch, celebrating each other's successes and welcoming visitors too.

The Newport Beachside Resort *(16701 Collins Ave., Sunny Isles Beach* ☎ *306/949-1300* ☎ *www.newportbeachsideresort.com)* sits on a vast swath of white sand beach lined with tall coconut palms and palapa huts, overlooking the Atlantic. All 300 rooms boast an ocean view. Everything from volleyball to shuffle board plus all the water sports are available here and five restaurants ensure you don't starve.

It helps to be bilingual in Miami – Spanish is widely spoken and a few words are sure to broaden the smiles of the Latino expatriates whose establishments add so much colour and joie de vivre. And it helps to be beautiful since almost everybody in Miami, male or female, seems to be knock-down gorgeous.

Sandra Peic

Sandra Peic is Art Director/Designer of Florida, Eh?

Florida's Deep South
World eco-treasures at risk

The Keys – Ocean, reef and islands

Geography alone is a dandy excuse for investigating the Florida Keys. That long skinny string of islands and coral reefs, stretching far into the ocean toward Cuba, connected by 123 miles of fragile highway, is a spectacular drive and, in stormy weather, a daunting one. Our first experience of that drive, eons ago, was during a ferocious rain and wind storm, driving a tall box-shaped motor home that lurched crazily with every gust. Getting there was half the fun, as VIA Rail used to say.

But this time, the sun shone on a tranquil azure sea. The palms bowed gracefully in soft breezes, the bougainvillea splashed themselves all over fences and houses – it was the picture of paradise.

Yet that idyllic image, backed up by all the Keys' hype about eco-tourism, belies the real danger that faces this unique and fragile environment as more tourists, generating more pollution, descend in ever-greater numbers. The Keys' greatest treasure, its 320-km.off-shore coral reef, a treasure built over thousands of years, home to thousands of fish and plants, is endangered. Recent reports that 85 per cent of its delicate elkhorn coral is already dead, probably killed by human sewage dumped from boats and spilled from septic tanks, is a message that shouldn't be ignored. Better education, backed up by stricter regulations and stiffer penalties are urgently needed.

And wouldn't it be great if some bright entrepreneur reinstated the old Flagler rail line – which until the thirties linked Jacksonville with the Keys

Dive in to the Amoray Dive Resort at Key Largo, almost too pretty to leave for a day underwater.

and now serves joggers, bikers and fisherfolk – as a luxury Miami-to-Key West train ride, thus eliminating at least some car emissions.

Despite the risk, eco-tourism ranks right up there with 'round-the-clock partying as the Keys' premiere activity. It begins near Key Largo at **John Pennekamp Coral Reef State Park** (the only park in all of Florida where we encountered a rude park ranger) which stretches across several miles of reef, delighting divers, snorkellers and glass bottom boat buffs. The ecological wonders extend all the way to the Dry Tortugas, 70 miles beyond Key West. At every step of the way, outfitters and tour operators are waiting to show you the stunning riches that land and sea have provided.

Lush tropical foliage contrasts with the Keys' white sands and blue waters.

Key Largo abuts **Everglades National Park**, with myriad wilderness options. Nearby, the **Crocodile Lake National Wildlife Refuge**, is a nesting area for crocodiles which, unlike alligators, are rare in Florida, and the five-acre **Wild Bird Center**, a nursing home for injured native and migratory birds.

Amy Slate's Amoray Dive Resort ✪ ($$-$$$) ✪ 104250 Overseas Hwy., Key Largo 33037 ✪ 1-800-426-6729 ✪ www.amoray.com

This friendly and unpretentious resort caters to divers with a 45-foot dive/snorkel boat waiting at the dock to transport divers to all the premier spots in the nearby National Marine Park Sanctuary, dive masters on site, and diving certification programs available. The resort's 25 air conditioned rooms and apartments are decorated in island pastels with white wicker furniture, fully equipped kitchens and a screened dining porch. Continental breakfast, use of kayaks and snorkel gear are included in the price and there is a popular restaurant two doors away. The resort does not accept pets, campers or trailers. There's a well-stocked shop with all the perks and accessories that divers need. Special packages are offered along with discounts for returning students.

Windley Key Fossil Reef , Hwy. 1, Islamorada

Amateur geologists will revel in **Windley Key Fossil Reef**, (Hwy.1, Mile 106), a state geological site just east of Islamorada. Key Largo limestone was quarried here to build Flagler's railway and bridges and to ship north for decorative keystones on fine public buildings. The quarry remained active until the 1960s. Now its steep walls and remaining blocks of stone reveal a dazzling array of ancient coral creatures. Walking trails – the longest is half a mile – reveal some 40 varieties of trees and a recently

Once a rock quarry, Windley Key displays machinery and blocks of fossil-rich stone.

planted butterfly garden supports each stage of the butterfly's life. Watch for swallowtails, gossamer-wings, whites and sulphurs, skippers and many more. At the pleasant new visitor centre, super-helpful park rangers and compact trail guide booklets provide plenty of information about butterflies, fossils and wildlife. Open 8-5, Thurs-Mon. Adults $1.50, kids under six free. Guided tours $2.50.

A few miles further west, **Lignumvitae Key State Park and Botanical Site** awaits, a mile off-shore, accessible only by water and toured only with a park ranger. The Keys are bursting at the seams with development. So finding an island that has escaped 'progress' is a special treat. We hopped aboard a tour boat from **Robbie's Marina**, (Mile 77.5 near Islamorada), for the six-minute bats-outa-hell voyage.

The island has never been harvested, burned, lumbered or gardened. New York financier William Matheson bought the 280 acre island in the early 1900s for $1 'and other valuable considerations' (not spelled out) and built a limestone house for his caretakers. He and his family visited aboard their yacht.

The old house, furnished in authentic 1919 style, has an ice box, wood stove and water pump. A diesel generator now supplies power, once supplied by a windmill. Water comes from an 11,000-gallon rainwater tank – the island has no other water source.

Our ranger, Steve, led us along broad pathways through ancient forests, pointing out poisonwood trees, which are like poison ivy to the nth degree, sapadillo, which produces chickle for chewing gum, and mastic, with fruit so sticky that even raccoons avoid it. But lignumvitae trees, credited with amazing curative powers, and still used in modern medications, are rare on the island that bears their name.

Back on the mainland, **Robbie's Marina** offers an engrossing view of nature. For $2, you can buy a bucket of fish to feed hordes of voracious tarpon, waiting along the dock, competing with equally voracious pelicans who sometimes beat them to the catch. The pelicans are unwelcome – visitors are asked not to feed them – but there's a helper, a lean black and white sheep dog who races up and down the dock, herding the pelicans away from the guests. The pelicans are patient, the dog is persistent . . . the game is endless. Periodically, the dog collapses in a sleepy pile, heedless of passing feet, only to leap up again in a few minutes to continue his chores.

In an elegant pose, writer Isobel Warren feeds the hungry tarpon at Robbie's Marina.

The Hungry Tarpon ✺ *Hwy. 1, 77522 Overseas Hwy., Islamorada 33036* ✺ *305-665-0535* ✺ *www.hungrytarpon.com*

The Hungry Tarpon is a tiny old-style diner beside the highway at Robbie's Marina. Here the Bond family serves up hearty and delicious lunches and dinners to fortify fishermen and road warriors. Their 'grits and grunts' breakfast comprising a mountain of grits, biscuits, eggs and fried fish, with plenty of coffee and juice, or the huge veggie burrito stuffed with savory scrambled eggs, mushrooms, tomatoes and onions, topped with spicy green salsa and served with a bowl of grits, each cost about $10. Lunches are similarly huge, tasty and inexpensive. We sampled the grilled fish sandwich with lettuce, tomatoes and cheese, on excellent bread, lightly grilled and flattened. Is it healthy? One of the restaurant's many amusing signs says it best: **Eat well, stay fit, die anyway!** It's open from 6:30 a.m. to 3.

Marathon

This busy little city marks the mid-point of the Keys, just short of the **Seven Mile Bridge**. Less

Birds vs. dog – one pooch's never-ending mission to rid the dock of pelicans.

crowded and less expensive than Key West, which is about an hour away, it serves as headquarters for innumerable tour and fishing charter boats.

Cocoplum Beach and Tennis Club ❂ *($$-$$$$)* ❂ *109 Cocoplum Dr., Marathon FL 33050* ❂ *1-800-228-1587* ❂ *www.cocoplum.com. Mile 54.5*

Right at the ocean's edge, these 20 unusual octagonal villas are set among palm and fruit trees. Each two-bedroom, two-bathroom home includes a living room, kitchen, dining room, and wrap-around screened porch, the two upper floors connected by a spiral staircase.

Sunrise gave us a rich pink sky, glowing across the sea. To the west, a full moon still hung in the sky. A flotilla of pelicans flew low over the water, breakfast-shopping and a school of fish boiled to the surface. Suddenly at water's edge, a great white heron promenaded splendidly down the beach, just a few feet from our balcony, silhouetted against the pink sea and framed by palm fronds. It was an unforgettable moment.

Cocoplum is the ultimate laid-back resort, handy to everything that the Keys have to offer – sport fishing, scuba and snorkeling expeditions, sailing, kayaking, and of course, Key West, some 60 miles (96 km) away. On site there's a well-kept tennis court and the white sand beach where hammocks are slung from the palm trees. We even enjoyed fresh bananas, straight from the management's trees. Long-stays qualify for up to 30 per cent discounts.

Pigeon Key

Just before the **Seven Mile Bridge, Pigeon Key**, a five-acre island that housed workers building the Flagler railroad between 1905 and 1912, and maintenance crews until a vicious 1935 hurricane demolished portion of track. Beset by Depression woes, the Florida East Coast Railroad

Cocoplum Resort's spacious octagonal cottages, with plenty of space for families, rise three stories to provide a fine view of the ocean.

sold its right-of-way to the state of Florida and it was converted to a two-lane highway. The University of Miami used the site for marine research until, in 1992, The Pigeon Key Foundation raised money and resources to restore the site, now on the National Register of Historic Places, and to mount programs of environmental education and marine research for day visitors or long-stay groups. *Pigeon Key Foundation* ✪ *305-289-0025* ✪ *www.pigeonkey.org*

Big Pine Key at Mile 30 is home to tiny white tail deer which can often be spied, especially at dawn or dusk, in the **National Key Deer Refuge**. But look, don't touch – visitors are asked not to feed or pet the deer.

Key West

The first lesson we'll share about Key West is this: Never visit during March break, unless of course, you're a student. Then you'll have a blast.

In fact, the town's party atmosphere is legendary, especially at sunset when le beau monde gathers at Mallory Square to drink, dance, play and cheer departing Sol.

It continues year-round with parties and festivals, highlighted by **Fantasy Fest** (www.fantasyfest.net) in late October, a 10-day extravaganza of costumes, masquerade balls, street fairs and parades. All winter long, **Old Island Days** include art and craft shows, music and theatre and even a conch shell blowing contest.

The home of author **Ernest Hemingway,** who did time at the Toronto Telegram before departing for warmer climes is an interesting museum. (907 Whitehead St., Adults, $8, children under 12, $5. Open 9-5). The **Mel Fisher Museum** (200 Greene St., Adults $6.50, children $3. Open 9:30-5:30) is a collection of maritime and shipwreck antiquities. **Audubon House** (205 Whitehead St., Adults, $8.50, children $3.50. Open 9:30-5.) showcases the works of John James Audubon who visited the area in 1832.

And so to sleep

Key West accommodations can be pricey – day trips from locations further up the Keys may coddle your budget. However, the recent downturn in travel has prompted some deals, such as extra free nights, reduced room rates and credits for dining and spa treatments.

The Bottle Inn in Key West is decorated with – you guessed it – bottles!

Frances Street Bottle Inn ✪ 535 Frances St Key West, FL 33040
✪ *1-800-294-8530* ✪ *www.bottleinn.com*

Far from the madding crowds of Duval Street but close enough to stroll over and observe the shenanigans, the gracious Bottle Inn is a grand old house, ringed by a deep shady verandah, with bright airy rooms and in the lobby, hand-painted furniture in vivid hues.

Each evening, a social hour with drinks and hors d'oeuvres helps guests get acquainted as does the eight-person hot tub in the courtyard. Mary Beth and Jim McCulloch turned their backs on corporate careers up north to become innkeepers in 1997. Both collectors of bottles and glass, they purchased an inn with a built-in collection of more of the same. Now they have some 500 bottles on display and as many more in storage. Each room has its bottles and the windows are lined with rich cobalt blue, deep green, pale green and brown bottles, many of them salvaged from Key West Harbour. Built in 1926, the house did time as a church, a boarding house and in 1992 the set of the Meteor Newspaper offices in the TV series, 'Key West'.

Rainbow flag welcomes visitors at Pearl's Rainbow, a friendly Key West inn for women only.

Pearl's Rainbow ✪ *($$-$$$)* ✪ *525 United St., Key West, FL 33040* ✪ *1-800-749.6696* ✪ *www.pearlsrainbow.com*

Key West is a gay-friendly city and the rainbow flag flies at Pearl's Rainbow, an inn especially for women. Owners Leslie Leonelli and Heather Carruthers abandoned Manhattan for Key West, to create a private and secure haven.

The rooms are immaculate and simple, with white furniture, pastel walls and private baths. Some have

Sandy beach, calm ocean, fishing poles, hammocks and palm trees – a recipe for relaxation at Cocoplum Resort, Marathon.

private balconies. Outside, there are two pools, a hot tub, an open-air massage room under a canvas canopy and a poolside bar and grill. Breakfast, included in the room rate, runs to fruits, yogurt, cereals, juice and coffee. Community kitchens (shared by only three or four rooms) enhance both social life and budget.

Nearly 10 per cent of the inn's clientele are Canadian. Discounts of up to 20 per cent (depending on season) are offered on long-term stays. The inn arranges monthly dances, 'Learn to Scuba' weekends, and women-only snorkeling, fishing and dolphin-watching trips. All women, aged 18 or over, are welcome.

Florida Keys is on line at www.fla-keys.com

Bluewater Key RV Resort ✪ *($$$)* ✪ *2950 US Hwy 1, Key West FL 33040* ✪ *www.bluewaterkey.com*

This 81-site resort 10 miles (16 km) from Key West rents to transient RVers when the owners are absent. Set within the Saddlebunch Keys, the resort is surrounded by water. Waterfront sites face the water, while canal, poolside and offwater sites may have partial water views. But no site is more than 100 feet from the water.

There's fishing off the 100-foot dock and the coral reef just offshore invites snorkeling and scuba diving. A hike and bike trail runs several miles along the water and golf and tennis are available within a few miles.

Minimum RV length is 26 feet and no tents, pop-ups or truck campers are allowed. Open year-round, 9-4.

The Sinking of the Spiegel Grove

It's a tale worthy of Gordon Lightfoot or perhaps Rick Mercer – the sinking of the Spiegel Grove, a 520-foot retired U.S. Navy ship, scuttled in 130 feet of water, six miles off Key Largo, to create a massive artificial reef in the Florida Keys National Marine Sanctuary. But in a seascape riddled with wrecks, this ship refused to sink. Or rather, it sank on its own terms, despite all the efforts of the 'experts' who sought to guide it. En route to its final resting grounds, the ship rolled on its side and sank, leaving its bow sticking up out of the sea. That meant extensive – and expensive – three-week salvage operations that began with air injection to remove water from the hull, 70 inflatable lift bags to provide about 500 tons of buoyancy, then two tugboats, providing 100 tons of pull, assisted by the ocean current, to roll it over. Preparing the ship for sinking had already cost more than $1 million and 28,000 man hours of cleaning to remove residual petroleum products, peeling paint, asbestos and other possible contaminants. But that wasn't enough. When the ship finally went down, sort of, the drama continued. A 'petroleum-like sheen', five feet wide and several hundred yards long, began to spread across the water. Before the site could open to divers, the leak had to be found and fixed.

Destined to be a Florida Keys dive site, the Spiegel Grove sank too soon, requiring costly salvage operations.

The Everglades – Saving the 'River of Grass'

Remember all those jokes about gullible Northerners buying an acre of Florida swamp – or better still 100 acres? Not long ago, Florida swampland was deemed useless – fit only for scamming knuckleheads and draining for development. Fortunately all that has changed – and not a moment too soon.

It's estimated that more than half the Everglades wetlands and thousands of bird, animal and aquatic species have already succumbed to development – but finally efforts are underway to save what is left. The 1,700 miles of canals and levees built to redirect Everglades water into the Atlantic (some 1.7 million gallons drain into the ocean daily) are now under scrutiny. The $7.8 billion Comprehensive Everglades Restoration Plan will close many canals, returning the water flow to the 'River of Grass' where it belongs. Southern Florida's hunger for water – for golf courses, swimming pools and luxury resorts – is unabated, however. The Everglades restoration may be short lived.

Ah-Tah-Thi-Ki Museum is component of both day and overnight tours that explore Seminole history.

Though substantial tracts of the Everglades and their wildlife have been lost, this vast wilderness still dominates southern Florida, from the Kissimmee lakes to Florida Bay – some five million acres, mostly designated as parks. **Everglades National Park** alone claims 1.5 million acres. To the north there's the 720,000-acre **Big Cypress National Preserve**, next to the **Big Cypress Indian Reservation** and at the eastern entrance to the Keys, **Biscayne National Park** with 172,000 acres. The eco-opportunities are boundless.

Flamingo Lodge, at Everglades' southern tip, rents all types of watercraft, including houseboats, for exploring the 'River of Grass.'

Seminole Tours ✪ *305-257-3737* ✪ *www.floridaeco-tours.com*

Fort Lauderdale adjoins the Everglades near **Big Cypress Swamp**, traditional home of the Seminole Tribe which offers tours that overnight in screened chickee (that's Seminole for house) cabins on the reservation. Tours include the **Ah-Tah-Thi-Ki Museum** with its displays and interpretive exhibits, then a swamp buggy and airboat ride at the **Billie Swamp Safari**. A reptile show, campfire with Indian storytelling and night time swamp buggy eco-tour are included. Tours are about $110 for adults, $50 for children.

The **Swampwater Café** at the **Billie Swamp Safari Park** (863-983-6101 ✪ www.seminoletribe.com/safari) serves alligator, catfish, frybread and Indian tacos.

The Ah-Tah-Thi-Ki Museum ✪ *5845 S. State Road 7, Ft. Lauderdale 33314* ✪ *863-902-1113* ✪ *www.seminoletribe/museum* ✪ *Open Tues-Sun, 9-5. Adm: adults $6, kids and seniors $4.*

Florida's Seminole Indians maintain a vibrant presence in the Everglades. The **Ah-Tah-Thi-Ki Museum**, on the **Big Cypress Reservation**, 17 miles north of Everglades Parkway, explains the tribe's history and culture with excellent displays and exhibits, plus a five-screen video presentation. Life-size dioramas, the figures clothed in the colourful costumes of a century ago, capture dramatic elements of Seminole life such as the green corn dance. A mile-long nature boardwalk that's wheelchair accessible provides close-up glimpses of swamp and forest with excellent plant identification's all along the way. At the boardwalk's furthest point, a few craftspeople exhibit traditional skills – canoe building, beadwork and quilting.

Everglades National Park ❂ *State Rd. 9336, Homestead 33034* ❂ *305-242-7700* ❂ *www.nps.gov/ever/* (Adm. $10 per car) has been named a World Heritage Site, an International Biosphere Reserve, and a Wetland of International Importance. From the entrance near **Homestead**, south of Miami, Hwy. 9336 meanders 38 miles (61 km) west and south to **Flamingo**, the southernmost point. The visitor centre at Homestead provides an excellent introduction with displays, videos and knowledgeable park rangers while nearby Royal Palm Hammock offers two half-mile nature trails. Hiking, biking, canoeing, backcountry camping, fishing and airboat riding are popular ways to explore the park.

Flamingo Lodge Marina and Outpost Resort ❂ *($-$$)* ❂ *State Rd 9336, Flamingo, FL 33034* ❂ *1-800-600-3813* ❂ *www.flamingolodge.com*

The park's only overnight accommodations, this lodge on Florida Bay offers cabins, cottages, campsites, chickees and even houseboats. Canoes and kayaks are also available. A restaurant and screened café adjoin the lodge. The gift shop exhibits an understandable preoccupation with alligators. You find them on T-shirts, mugs, cups, and even in those time-honoured snowballs, substituting gold glitter for snow.

The lodge usually offers various money-saving packages, some during summer months (a season blessed with Kamikaze mosquitoes of formidable size and appetite so take gallons of repellent) and others during winter's slower periods.

House boats are an appealing option. You bring only your food, drink and fishing tackle – linens and galley gear are supplied. You don't need boating experience to drive one of these jalopies – their high speed is eight knots – but you do receive a thorough orientation course before departure, and detailed charts of the two routes that can be followed. Your major problem may be running aground, in which case the patient park staff come and haul you out. The boats

Robert is Here, starring Robert Moehling, is a fruit stand and then some.

sleep six to eight people, and should be reserved six months in advance, even earlier for Christmas and New Years. They may be booked through the lodge or at www.nps.gov.

Robert is Here ✪ *34815 Country Club Rd., Homestead 33034* ✪ *305-246-1592* ✪ *www.robertishere.com*

Follow the signs to Robert Is Here, a fruit stand like no other. Proprietor **Robert Moehling** claims to have a cult following. After you've tasted his milk shakes, you'll know why.

This sprawling fruit stand-cum-strawberry farm-cum-entertainment centre near the turn-off to the Everglades park, stars its owner – big, beaming, hard-working Robert Moehling who at age seven began selling produce by the roadside under his father's hand-lettered sign stating "Robert is Here." It worked. At 14, he bought his first house, 10 acres of land and a car and now owns the huge fruit stand (closed November and December) a ship-anywhere service specializing in tropical fruit, a turtle exhibit, and 65 acres of farmland. Along with fruits and veggies, some local, some imported, you'll find local honey – consider tangerine or avocado – along with sauces, dressings (try the key lime/mustard salad dressing), jams and jellies.

But back to those milkshakes – tasting is believing. We sampled the papaya/key lime

World's tiniest post office? Could be. It's at Ochopee on the Tamiami Trail.

blend but there are dozens more at $3 to $3.50 each – every fruit flavour you can think of, singly or in blends. They're a meal in themselves – including double dessert – huge and thick as ice cream. (Both a spoon and a straw are supplied.)

The **Tamiami Trail** (Tampa-to-Miami, in case the name puzzles you) cuts across the Everglades, revealing many unsung treasures.

Development has destroyed many species but fortunately much wildlife remains in the Everglades.

Clyde Butcher's Big Cypress Gallery, *42388 Tamiami Trail, Ochopee, FL 34141* ☼ *941-695-2428* ☼ *www.clydebutcher.com* exhibits the work of this award-winning photographer who for 30 years has trained his lens on Florida's landscape. He also maintains a gallery in Venice, at 237 Warfield Ave., 941-486-0811.

Ochopee Post Office, 28 miles (45 km) southeast of Naples, may well be the world's smallest postal outlet and the only one occupying a recycled outhouse. The story goes that when the local general store, which included the post office, burned to the ground half a century ago, the good burghers of Ochopee commandeered a temporary site, an equipment storage shed that some wags say was an outhouse. Whatever . . . it's still the post office. If you arrive during business hours you can have your letters hand-stamped with the Ochopee stamp. Mail dropped in the outside box gets the standard U.S. postmark.

The **Panther Gift Shop,** 30 miles southeast of Naples, is another Tamiami Trail fixture. Here you'll hear about the skunk ape, a legendary swamp creature rather like an Everglades version of Canada's Sasquatch. The illusive skunk ape, which resembles an orangutan, lives in Big Cypress Swamp in a cypress dome – a cave enclosed by cypress trees – and appears only rarely, mostly to the owners of the Panther Gift Shop. Drop in for the whole story.

Joanie's Blue Crab Café ✪ *($)* ✪ *Tamiami Trail, 28 miles south-east (45 km) of Naples* ✪ *941-695-2682*

If you've never tasted 'gator nuggets, dig in. Joanie's are grilled, slightly chewy and served up with her spicey home-made salsas and Indian fried bread. Or try the swamp dinner for ' gator fritters and nuggets, frogs legs and fried bread. More conventional diners settle for oysters, shrimp or stone crab salad, sandwiches, burgers and key lime pie. Open 11-5 daily. Since each dish is individually prepared, old hands call ahead to place their orders. Joanie's food is excellent and so is the décor. The walls are decorated with original paintings of the Everglades, shell and found wood constructions, a massive rattle snake skin, alligator heads, funny sayings and post cards. If it were not the only restaurant for miles and miles on Highway 41, it would still be our first choice for its tasty fare and friendly service.

Everglades City ✪ *Hwy 29, south of the Tamiami Trail.*

It's easy to miss Everglades City but do pause at the well-stocked visitor centre at Highway 41 (the Tamiami Trail) and Highway 29 and drive just three miles south to this western gateway to the Everglades and launching point for many boat tours. Everglades City was named Florida Outstanding Rural Community of the Year in 1998.

The Museum of the Everglades (105 West Broadway, Everglades City FL 34139 ✪ *941-695-0008* ✪ *www.colliermuseum.com)* Photographs and artifacts trace 2000 years of human habitation in the southwest

Everglades safari tours stop at Joanie's Blue Crab Cafe, the only restaurant for miles on the Tamiami Trail, for tasty Everglades treats, such as 'gator nuggets and fried bread.

Alligators abound in the Everglades and tours provide opportunities for safe observation.

Everglades. It's housed in a former laundry that served workmen building the Tamiami Trail. Open Tues.-Sat., 11-4. Donation.

Everglades Spa-Fari ✪ *207 West Broadway, Everglades City, FL 34139* ✪ *941-695-1006* ✪ *www.spa-fari.com*

Cheryl Henderson used her retirement to become a licensed aesthetician and massage therapist. Now she has opened a new spa where she plans to offer the usual massages, facials and other treatments, as well as safaris into the Everglades.

And so to sleep …

Everglades Vacation Rentals ✪ *($$)* ✪ *201 W. Broadway, Everglades City FL 34139* ✪ *239-695-3151* ✪ *www.banksoftheeverglades.com*

In 1923 it was Collier County's first bank. Today it offers three-night, weekly and monthly stays, but this cleverly converted Historic Bank of the Everglades still looks like a bank – there's money scattered about, the safe is in the lobby, and adding machines and other monetary artifacts are everywhere. Its seven suites, each with sitting space, kitchen and bath, include the Foreclosure Department, Savings, Dividends and the Money Laundering Room, all comfortably furnished and, unlike banks, affordable too.

The bank has a chequered past. It weathered five hurricanes – including the vicious 1962 Hurricane Donna which dumped five feet of water on the vault floor. Innovative staff pinned more than a million dollars to a clothesline to dry, standing by through the night to prevent any unscheduled withdrawals.

The Everglades

Ivey House ✿ ($$) ✿ 107 Camillia St., Everglades City FL 34130 ✿ 941-695-3299 ✿ www.IveyHouse.com

The **Ivey House** is an attractive family-owned establishment encompassing a 17-room inn, open year-round and an 11-room B&B, which closes for the summer. In the spacious dining room, glass-topped tables display navigational charts of the Everglades. An all-day deli serves sandwiches, fruit and box lunches. Coffee, tea and cookies are complimentary all day long. The inn encircles a 30-foot 'conversation pool' – a huge hot tub, complete with jets, screened against mosquitoes. An interesting assortment of guided canoe tours and sightseeing trips into the Everglades is offered and canoes and bikes can be rented.

Everglades Safari ✿ 1-800-472-3069 ✿ www.ecosafari.com. Day safari, including lunch at Joanie's Blue Crab Café: Adults, $99.95; 60-plus, $89.95; kids under 12, $79.95. Reservations required.

Venture into the Everglades with a knowledgeable guide and the area's vital importance to both Florida's and the world's ecology comes brilliantly into focus. Hundreds of tours and safaris are available. Many will pick up at your hotel on either coast. Choosing is challenging but do investigate routes and programs, to ensure you're getting the depth of information you want. The mode of transport and the maximum number of participants is also relevant.

Airboat tours – noisy but fast – are a favourite means of traversing the 'River of Grass'.

We sampled the **Everglades Safari**, a 180-mile (289 km) day-long van circuit, beginning with a low-key boat ride through mangrove swamps.

You could say that when you've seen one mangrove you've seen 'em all, but the mangrove's first line of defence against nature is the focus here. The three mangrove varieties, black, white and red, all unrelated, form a kind of sea wall around Florida's southern tip, holding the soil and harbouring wildlife with their tangled roots.

Collier County information: 1-800-688-3600 ○ www.classicflorida.com

A lengthy hike into a cypress swamp in search of a 'gator hole revealed a mother who has laid claim to this pool for 15 years, with a couple of generations of young – she'll evict them when they're three years old.

In fact, we saw 'gators in profusion, from two-foot babies to 16-foot seniors – floating like logs or sunning themselves along man-made canals, and edging uncomfortably close as one ill-advised group wooed them with marshmallows. (Feeding alligators is illegal and liable to a substantial fine). Turtles and birds were also in evidence – the area is home to great white heron and blue heron, turkey and black vultures, quail, egrets, wild turkeys, deer and feral pigs.

The Florida panther, an elusive member of the cougar family, inhabits these vast preserves but he's rarely seen. Only about 70 remain and last year, our guide said, some 15 were killed by unheeding car drivers.

In fact, road kill is the primary cause of death for both panthers and black bear, another threatened species with only 1,500 remaining.

Tall wire fences punctuated with underpasses allow animals to cross safely under the highway.

An airboat ride, billed as the day's highlight turned out to be its low point for us as we roared through sawgrass and swamps, scaring the daylights out of any critter within miles of the racket and bombarding our ear drums in spite of protective cover.

Everglades - River of Grass

The 1947 book by journalist Marjory Stoneman Douglas wakened the world to the imminent loss of the unique Everglades eco-system. Along with many other outstanding books and videos, it's available by mail for US$6.95 from the Florida National Park and Monuments Association. **www.nps.gov/ever/fnpma.htm**

Parkwardens warn visitors. Approach wildlife– crocodiles and alligators, birds, snakes, raccoons and fish – with caution. Feeding alligators could cost you a heavy fine and maybe even your hand. Small children and dogs are dangerously close in size to an alligator's favourite snack. There are 26 species of snakes in southern Florida and four are venomous. Steer clear!

The Gulf Coast

The **Tamiami Trail** turns north at **Naples,** probably Florida's most affluent city. Naples prides itself on its pedestrian walks lined with fine shops, art galleries and restaurants. And powdery sand beaches marked by boardwalks across the dunes.

Immokalee – the name means 'my home' in Seminole – is still home to Seminole Indians. It's a cattle ranching and farming region, 35 miles (56 km) northeast of Naples. **Roberts Ranch** is now being developed as a museum of Collier County's early ranchers and farming families. Nearby is the **National Audubon Society's** 11,000-acre **Corkscrew Swamp Sanctuary**, home to hordes of alligators and endangered birds.

Marco Island, largest and northernmost of Southwest Florida's **Ten Thousand Islands**, is an upscale enclave of fine beaches, golf courses, shopping and dining. Shelling, birdwatching and beach combing are other pursuits.

Goodland (SR 92 on Marco Island, pop. 200), once a commercial fishing village, is a base for shallow water sport fishing. But its top attraction is **Stan's Idle Hour Seafood Restaurant and Bar**, the home of the 'Buzzard Lope', a new take on the Macarena.

Fort Myers

Entering **Fort Myers** isn't so much a drive as a procession – a grand entry if you will, thanks to McGregor Boulevard, the elegant main drag. For 15 miles (24 km), it's lined with towering royal palms – 1,800 of them – some planted by Thomas Edison whose fine estate is one of the major attractions here.

The Edison-Ford Winter Estates ✪ *2350 McGregor Blvd., Fort Myers* ✪ *239-334-7419* ✪ *www.edison-ford-estate.com*

Inventor **Thomas Edison** paid $2,750 in 1885 for a 13-acre parcel of land along the Caloosahatchee River, where he built the winter home and workplace that served until his death in 1931. Edison moved there for his health and lived to be 84, so the plan must have worked. The estate showcases his home, office, laboratory and experimental gardens, all carefully preserved. Many a famous name visited here and in 1916, Edison's pal, **Henry Ford**, bought the house next door so he could spend winters with his friends. The estates are a must-see in Fort Myers.

Edison's home boasted one of Florida's first swimming pools, and 'electroliers' – electric chandeliers, designed by Edison and hand made of brass in his own workshop. His laboratory, where a major project was extracting rubber from goldenrod, remains just as it was when he worked there. An artifact museum exhibits many of his inventions.

The botanical garden displays more than 1,000 varieties of plants, imported from

Fleet's in, nets are drying, at Beach Seafood Market, Fort Myers Beach.

around the world, including African sausage trees and a Banyan tree, a gift from **Harvey Firestone** in 1925. Now, with a girth of over 400 feet, it's the country's largest banyan. Originally an experimental garden for scientific research, the garden was later enhanced with Mrs. Edison's favourite roses, orchids and bromeliads.

Open daily except Thanksgiving and Christmas, Mon-Sat 9 to 4, Sun 12-4. Combined ticket for both estates: Adults $12, children $5.50.

Edison, Ford and their friend Harvey Firestone are permanently reunited in the city's eight-acre **Centennial Park** where a life-like bronze statue of the trio, "Uncommon Friends", sculpted by local artist D.J. Wilkins, is set within a fountain.

Fort Myers Historical Museum ✿ *2300 Peck St., Fort Myers* ✿ *239-332-5955* ✿ *www.cityftmyers.com/attractions/historical.htm*

Two-hour walking tours, laced with fascinating stories about the city and its architecture, are offered by the **Fort Myers Historical Museum** Wednesdays at 10 a.m. Reservations required. Adults $5, children $3; discount on museum entry. The museum occupies the restored **Atlantic Coastline Railroad Depot**, built in 1924. A key attraction is the Esperanza, a plush restored Pullman car from the 1930s. Tues-Sat: 9-4. Adults $6, seniors $5.50, kids 3-12 $3.

Phone numbers

Although many Florida inns advertise toll-free numbers, very few extend that courtesy to Canadians. As well, the state's telephone area codes are changing. We've done our best to provide current numbers, but these two factors may result in calls that can't be completed. Do remind innkeepers that Canadians comprise a huge market in Florida and the courtesy of a toll-free number is simply good business.

Eateries

Beach Seafood Market and Grill ✿ *($)* ✿ *1100 Shrimp Boat Lane, Fort Myers Beach.* ✿ *239-463-8777* ✿

If you want the best fish, find the fishing boats. And we did! A massive sign proclaiming 'SHRIMP' lured us south on Main Street, just before the San Carlos Blvd. causeway to **Fort Myers Beach**. And there, less than a kilometre away, we found the **Beach Seafood Market and Grill**.

And what a find – a place to buy, eat or

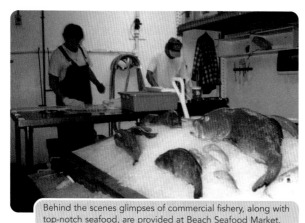

Behind the scenes glimpses of commercial fishery, along with top-notch seafood, are provided at Beach Seafood Market.

take away the freshest fish and seafood, caught offshore by the company's 17-boat fishing fleet. Two no-frills dining areas are separated by a counter of fresh seafood and a work area where manager Chick Eli and his helpers are filleting the day's catch – red or yellow-fin grouper, button or mangrove snapper and porgie which Chick de-clares an under-appreciated fish, and one of the tastiest. In the back dining room, you can view a video about shrimp fishing or watch the shrimp grading machines at work in the next room.

The menu is straightforward – shrimp, buffalo shrimp (hot and spicy), grouper, oysters or scallops with tasty fries and a big salad for $7.95. For carnivores there are hamburgers and hot dogs. The restaurant is open 11 to 5, the market 8 to 6:30.

A fringe benefit is Capt. Mallet (a.k.a. Don Petrie), a retired optometrist who has worked part-time at the market for 17 years and makes crab mallets, indispensable for cracking crab shells. It started as a hobby but these days, with the help of his wife, he turns out some 25,000 mallets a year, selling them to seafood restaurants. You can get an autographed copy at the Market for $2. Be sure to mention **'Florida, Eh?'**

The French Connection Café ✪ *($-$$)* ✪ *2282 First St., Fort Myers* ✪ *239-332-4443* ✪ hides a quiet haven with private booths, tiny tables and old-fashioned bentwood chairs behind a big noisy bar and billiard table. Take your pick. The atmosphere is casual and so is the menu, running to quiches and crepes with tasty desserts. Open 11am - 2 am, Mon-Sat.

Bara Bread Bistro and French Bakery ✪ *($)* ✪ *1520 Broadway* ✪ *239-334-8216* ✪ is a fabulous find, a European bakery café with good cappuccino, feather-light croissants, tempting pastries, a good range of sandwiches plus loaves, buns and take-away goodies, all in a high-ceilinged lemon yellow room sprinkled with café tables. The French breakfast offers tartines, croissant, coffee and juice at $5. Lunchtime salads and quiches cost $6. Open Tues-Fri 7-5, Sat-Sun 8-3.

(Right next door, **Shakespeare, Beethoven and Company**, 1520 Broadway, Ft. Myers * 239-332-8300 * is a book-aholic's delight with an excellent selection of books, magazines and music.)

Out and About

Cracker Cooking School ❂ *P.O. Box 60079, Fort Myers, FL 33906* ❂ *1-800-296-0249* ❂ *rptours@aol.com*

Don't worry – this school doesn't teach you to cook a cracker. Its name recalls the early 'crackers' – cowherds whose cracking whips rounded up wild cattle. The day-long junket along Rte. 29 starts at Gatorama, where 5,000 alligators are raised for their skins and meat, moves to a beekeeper to savour various honeys and visits a research grove, to sample oranges, grapefruit or whatever is in season. The day's highlight is lunch, demonstrated by Chef Buddy Taylor, a fourth generation Floridian who prepares a sumptuous spread of alligator tail, swamp cabbage, pork ribs, chicken, citrus-based dressings and marinades, and pinto rancheros. Topping it off is wild orange pie, a rival for key lime. Students can shop for rare ingredients and take recipes home. Available only to groups of 20, $69 pp, including lunch. Mon.-Fri., Oct.-May.

Babcock Wilderness Adventure ❂ *8000 S.R. 31, Punta Gorda 33982* ❂ *1-800-500-5583* ❂ *www.babcockwilderness.com*

The 90,000-acre Crescent B Ranch, north of Fort Myers, combines ranching lore and wildlife sightings in swamp buggy or off-road bike tours. The Gator Shack Restaurant offers light lunches, including Gator Bites. Tours Nov-May, 9 am and 3 pm., June-Oct., mornings only. Adults $17.95, children, 3-12 $9.95. Reservations required. The site also includes a museum and country store.

GAEA Guides ❂ *Fort Myers, FL 33905* ❂ *1-866-256-6388* ❂ *239-694-5513* ❂ *www.gaeaguides.com*

Connie Langmann is a professional naturalist leading kayak nature tours through the waterways of Lee County. With over 20 years of eco-experience, she's familiar with all the area's hidden places and bases each day's

Unique B&B, the Black Tie, an antique wooden vessel anchored in Fort Myers, did wartime duty as a training ship.

itinerary on winds, tides and wildlife. Her four to five hour jaunts penetrate back bays, wildlife refuges, mangrove forests, bayous and rivers to spy dolphins, alligators, otters, anhingas, ibis, osprey, roseate spoonbills and many other species. Groups are small – four to six people, singles or doubles, with a jump seat for the tads. GAEA picks up and delivers at hotels. Cost is $50 pp.

Yacht Black Tie B&B and Old Florida River Tours ✪ *($$)* ✪ *1300 Lee St., Fort Myers 33901* ✪ *239-826-2457* ✪ *www.OFRT.com*

The highlight of our Fort Myers visit was the Black Tie B&B and its master, Captain Conrad Brown. This vintage 60-foot wooden boat is anchored at the first slip in the Fort Myers City Yacht Basin and offers just two staterooms. Our forward stateroom had a queen length bed that curved round the hull, an antique leather reading chair and it's own library and satellite TV. The adjacent bathroom had a regular flush toilet, sink and shower, with plenty of hot water. In the compact galley, the refrigerator was packed with breakfast goodies. Chaise lounges on the sunny foredeck, chairs and benches and a thick pad for lolling on the roofed aft deck were a prescription for relaxation.

And it worked. Sitting at twilight with a frosty glass of white wine, aware of the boat's gentle roll, the lapping waves, the lights reflected on the

Captain Conrad, genial master of the Black Tie, offers day cruises plus B&B.

water, the sounds of traffic far away, there seemed no more perfect place in the world.

The Black Tie began life in 1936 as a 'bait boat' running errands for a San Diego fishing company. When the company swamped, a businessman scooped her up and had her refitted as a luxury yacht. Then came the war and the US navy nabbed her for training duties, returning her to her owner in disastrous condition. Again refurbished, she was shunted about the west coast before heading overland to Fort Myers, there to languish dockside, barely staying afloat. That's when Capt. Conrad found her and spent two hard years restoring the vessel to its antique glory.

This busy little ship has a day job too – cruises up the Caloosahatchee River, through the Franklin Lock and into the Old Florida landscape for just six passengers, plus captain and crew. This lazy all-day trip costs $120 pp, including lunch, taxes and gratuities. The itinerary bypasses beaches and shelling in favour of the old river's myriad wildlife. Reservations are essential.

Captain Conrad is a retired architect who spent years in the Caribbean, and holds a 100-ton U.S. Coast Guard Master license.

Li-Inn B&B, 2135 McGregor Blvd. ✪ *Fort Myers 33901* ✪ *239-332-2651*
✪ *www.cyberstreet.com/users/li-inn.htm*

The Lion Sleeps here and so can you, conveniently close to the Edison Museum. Jim Haas and his friendly Lassa Apsu, Holly, bought the inn in 1999. It's now a member of Florida's Superior Small Lodgings. The five guest rooms (one is wheelchair accessible) are fresh and bright, decorated in pastels with antique furniture. Some of them are paneled in now-rare Lee County heart pine. Jim's breakfasts include homemade scones and muffins, banana and chocolate chip pancakes. His co-host, Holly, is charming to guests of the human persuasion but territorial toward animals so there's a no-pets policy.

Mariner's Lodge ✪ *($-$$)* ✪ *17990 San Carlos Blvd., Fort Myers Beach, FL 33931* ✪ *1-800-211-9099* ✪ *www.marinerslodge.com*

This 34-unit inn, situated on a deep canal near the Gulf of Mexico, is already a popular spot for Canadians, many returning year after year. A Superior Small Lodgings member, it offers both standard rooms and efficiencies. There's a heated pool, whirlpool spa, guest laundry and fishing docks. With its own marina for guests' dockage, it's near the beach and state parks – Lover's Key and 'Ding' Darling Refuge on Sanibel Island.

Country Inn and Suites ✪ *13901 Shell Point Plaza, Fort Myers, FL 33908* ✪ *239-454-9292* ✪ *www.countryinns.com/sanibelfl_gateway*

No surprises but well appointed lodgings with plenty of perks – that's the story at Country Inn & Suites, just three miles from the Sanibel Causeway. With 112 rooms and suites, it offers an outdoor pool, exercise room, guest laundry and complimentary breakfast. The hotel is set within palm-studded gardens, newly planted when we visited and promising to be ravishing once they've matured. It was interesting to see crop-topped young palms propped up by two by fours to withstand winds and weather.

Right next door, an outlet mall features well known labels such as Gap, Bass, Geoffrey Beene, Jones New York, Reebok, Van Heusen, Liz Claiborne, OshKosh B'Gosh, Naturalizer and Samsonite.

One of Sanibel's two theatres, this 1896 schoolhouse has been converted to a community theatre.

Sanibel and Captiva – Where the shells are

These offshore islands are beloved for their snowy beaches and exquisite shells, their wildlife sanctuaries and relaxed upscale ambience – even

car drivers are more courteous here than elsewhere in Florida. So eco-conscious are the islands that more than half their land is preserved as wildlife sanctuaries and building bylaws prohibit any building taller than the tallest palm tree.

Sanibel's principal thoroughfare, Periwinkle Way, is shaded by Australian pines and lined with galleries, restaurants and two theatres. It leads past the **J.N. 'Ding' Darling National Wildlife Refuge**, which has walking and canoe trails and a five-mile drive, and on to **Captiva**, which is even more laid-back and less populated.

Sanibel Library's soaring lobby displays collections of shells and fossils, all carefully labelled.

Sanibel's two theatres are the *Old Schoolhouse, 1905 Periwinkle Way* ☎ *239-472-6862* ☯ *www.old-schoolhousetheater.com* ☯ a tiny community playhouse in a one-room 1896 school, and the *J. Howard Wood Theatre, 2200 Periwinkle Way* ☯ *239-472-0006* ☯ *www.thewoodtheatre.com* ☯ a smart new facility in which no seat is further than 15 feet from the stage, mounting London and Broadway plays and musicals.

The Shell Game

Some 400 species of shells wash ashore on **Lee County's** 100 coastal islands and shelling is both a profession and a hobby, producing postures known as the Sanibel Slouch and the Captiva Crouch. Real zealots are out before dawn, flashlights strapped to foreheads, scooping up the tide's treasures.

But there's a rule – if it's alive, leave it. Harvesting shells that contain live creatures is prohibited though there's no limit on uninhabited shells.

Bailey-Matthews Shell Museum ✲ *3075 Sanibel-Captiva Road, Sanibel* ✲ *239-395-2233* ✲ www.shellmuseum.org ✲ Tues-Sun 10-4. Adults $5, Ages 8-16, $3, 7 and under, free. Perhaps the only museum in North America dedicated exclusively to seashells, this facility includes impressive educational exhibits and rare specimens from around the world. Experts can provide information and answer questions and there's a gift shop for those who would rather shop than stoop.

She Sells Sea Shells ✲ *1157 Periwinkle Way or 2422 Periwinkle Way, Sanibel* ✲ *239-472-6991* ✲ sells all manner of shells and shell-based décor and jewelry. They'll ship anywhere.

Sanibel Public Library ✲ *770 Dunlop Rd.* ✲ *239-472-2483* ✲ www.sanlib.org ✲ is worth a visit, just for the shell and fossil collection. And of course you may linger for the high-speed Internet access (not easy to find in Florida), or even better, the screened reading rooms, with ceiling fans and comfy rockers, overlooking quiet waterways.

The lobby of this handsome newish building displays 120 Lee County marine fossils, some of them thousands of years old, some representing species that date back five million years. There's also a camel's tooth, revealing that camels (paleolama) roamed this land in the Pleistocene age, before crossing the Bering Straits to Asia. The library's broad front windows exhibit dozens of fabulous shells that have washed ashore here. Both displays are carefully labelled.

The pleasant West Wind Inn is located on the quiet side of Sanibel near the J.N. 'Ding' Darling Sanctuary.

Lazy Flamingo Seafood, ✪ *($-$$)* ✪ *6520 Pine Ave. or 1036 Periwinkle Way, Sanibel Island* ✪ *239-472-6939* ✪ *www.lazyflamingo.com*

This Flamingo may be lazy but it has a hearty appetite. Our lunchtime servings were so large we didn't eat again until the next day. One consolation – a two-tier concoction of steamed mussels and clams, two dozen in all, probably burned more calories in prying open the shells than we actually consumed. Servings are huge. For the non-fishy, there's chicken, beef and burgers. They'll also cook your catch – mesquite grilled, plain grilled or sautéed, with fries and all the trimmings, for $7.95. This kid-friendly place with a pub-style ambience claims "If our seafood were any fresher, we would be serving it under water." Open daily, 11:30 am-1 am.

Where to sleep

The West Wind Inn ✪ *($$$-$$$$)* ✪ *3345 W. Gulf Drive, Sanibel Island, FL 33957* ✪ *1-800-824-0476* ✪ *www.westwindinn.com*

Elegant gardens with fountains and statuary invite relaxation at Sanibel's West Wind Inn.

This handsome property overlooks the Gulf of Mexico at the quiet end of Sanibel, not far from the J.N. 'Ding' Darling Wildlife Refuge. Each room has a screened lanai or balcony and all are equipped with either refrigerators or full kitchenettes. There's complimentary tennis (equipment supplied) and a butterfly garden with koi pond. The restaurant opens for breakfast and lunch all week, dinner on Friday and Saturday. The pool bar serves lunches and drinks. Check the website for numerous bargain-priced packages

Sun, sand, sea and the company of seabirds – all you need for a Sanibel holiday.

'Tween Waters Inn ❂ *($$$-$$$$)* ❂ *15951 Captiva Rd., Captiva Island FL 33924* ❂ *239-472-5161* ❂ *1-800-223-5865* ❂ *www.tween-waters.com*

Aviator **Charles Lindbergh** slept here. So did **Teddy Roosevelt**, ornithologist **Roger Tory Peterson** and many other famous folk.

Lee Island Coast information ❂ **1-888-231-6933**
❂ **www.LeeIslandCoast.com**

Opened in 1926, the inn recently restored six one-bedroom cottages that hosted famous names in the 20s, 30s, and 40s. Lindbergh's cottage reflects his aviation career. Roosevelt's passion for fishing shows in his decor while Peterson's features birds. Period fittings, such as claw foot tubs, paddle fans and working fireplaces accent the historic ambience.

The resort also includes standard rooms and suites, an Olympic sized pool, tennis, marina and rentals for boats, canoes and kayaks plus three dining rooms – the Old Captiva House, The Crow's Nest Lounge with casual dining and live entertainment and the waterfront Canoe & Kayak restaurant.

The resort hosts several **'tennis tune-ups'** yearly – five-day packages that include tennis clinics, drills and games, four nights' lodging, breakfast and lunch daily.

Sarasota

Sheltered by offshore islands that stretch from **Siesta Key** in the south to **Anna Maria Island** in the north, these neighbouring cities are strikingly different – Sarasota, a culture-vulture's heaven, Bradenton rich in down-home pleasures and wilderness.

Sarasota, with just 60,000 souls plus 150,000 in the surrounding county, supports a range of theatrical and artistic initiatives that puts to shame mighty Toronto, with 10 times the population.

The John and Mable Ringling Museum of Art ✪ 5401 Bay Shore Rd., Sarasota, FL 34243 ✪ 941-359-5700 ✪ www.ringling.org ✪ Adm.: $15.

Circus impresario John Ringling was no clown. In fact he was an astute businessman who made a fortune in real estate, railroads and the family circus, and spent it on a cultural treasure trove that he bequeathed to the people of Florida.

The Ringling estate comprises the art museum, the 32-room Ringling mansion and a circus museum, all within 66 manicured acres overlooking Sarasota Bay.

Ringling built the **Art Museum** in 1929 to house his vast collection. Its 21 galleries, which encircle a fabulous sculpture garden, are packed with over 10,000 objects ranging through paintings, sculptures, 25 huge

Ringling mansion, part of the huge Ringling Museum, is a Venetian-inspired fantasy, recently restored to its original 1926 opulence.

tapestries and various decorative arts. Its collections continue to grow; a contemporary gallery was added in 1966.

Ca d'Zan – which means 'House of John' in Venetian dialect – has recently undergone extensive renovations. This Venetian-inspired fantasy of towers and turrets, terraces and courtyards, was built in 1926. An 8,000-sq.-ft. marble terrace with 13 marble steps leads down to the Gulf of Mexico to welcome guests arriving by boat. (Ringling's yacht was moored there; his wife's gondola was docked on a tiny island that washed away in a 1926 hurricane.) Inside the litany of treasures continues – hand-painted cypress ceilings, floors of teak, oak and marble and luxurious furnishings, 95 per cent of them originals.

Atlas carries on – a spectacular garden accent at Sarasota's Ringling mansion.

The Circus Museum traces the history of the American circus – the first one was staged in Philadelphia in 1793 – with handbills and art prints, props, costumes and circus equipment, including beautifully carved parade and utility wagons. A detailed diorama provides an absorbing miniature view of all three rings of the 'big top' in action, complete with dancing bears, high wire artists, trained horses, wild animals, an excited audience and a uniformed band plus auxiliary tents filled with animals.

Van Wezel Performing Arts Hall ✪ *777 N. Tamiami Trail, Sarasota 34236* ✪ *1-800-826-9303* ✪ *www.vanwezel.org*

Once derided as 'the purple people seater', the spectacular Van Wezel theatre is a vast purple seashell, perched beside the sea. And it really is purple. We're not talking mere accents, folks, we're talking roof, walls (inside and out), carpets, seats, programs. But not the green room – it's beige. The effect is forceful and as eccentric as the man behind the design, architect Frank Lloyd Wright, and his widow, Olgivanna Wright, whose rare purple seashell (now displayed in a glass case in the foyer), inspired both the colour and the shell-like design elements.

A purple seashell inspired both colour and design of Sarasota's Van Wezel theatre, where Canadians often perform.

At the helm is **John Wilkes**, a Canadian who had already made his mark at Ontario Place, Toronto's O'Keefe and Dalhousie Arts Centre before 'landing in paradise' (his own words) in 1987 as general manager of Sarasota's premiere theatre. Under his leadership, the theatre has continued to broaden its scope with an eclectic mix of artistic tastes and genres.

The theatre's vast stage can accommodate full-scale operas, ballets and Broadway shows, but its programs reach out to all tastes – from rock, to jazz, to pops, to solo performers like Hal Holbrook. Canadian performers have always been prominent in the Van Wezel's line-up – Anne Murray, Paul Anka and the Royal Winnipeg Ballet, among others.

On summer Fridays, audiences arrive bearing deck chairs to hear jazz and lighter music from the terrace overlooking the gulf.

Asolo Theatre Company, The Mertz Theatre ❂ *5555 N. Tamiami Trail Sarasota 34243* ❂ *941-351-8000* ❂ *www.asolo.org*

This beautifully restored gem was originally an opera house, opened in Dunfermline, Scotland in 1903, and transplanted to Sarasota in 1990 to become part of the **Florida State University Center for the Performing Arts. The Asolo Theare Company** presents four different shows weekly in repertory, ranging from Shakespeare to Shaw to Noel Coward to

Agatha Christie. The Asolo also sponsors an innovative summer camp for disabled teens and young adults, a fertile creative process that now sees the 18 participants, writing, directing and performing their own shows.

Alongside, the neat little **June B. Cook Theater**, 162 seats in an intimate black box setting, is part of the **Asolo Conservatory for Actor Training**. It showcases the acting, directing and writing skills of graduate level student actors. You may catch a classic here but you'll also encounter ultra-contemporary works that fly in the face of theatre convention.

Marie Selby Botanical Gardens

Nine acres overlooking Sarasota Bay, some 20,000 exotic plants and a rainforest canopy make this a garden worth visiting. See 'Gardens' page 176 for details.

Where to eat

Captain Brian's Seafood Market Restaurant ✪ ($-$$) ✪ 8441 North Tamiami Trail, Sarasota. ✪ 941-351-4492

More good seafood, this time on Hwy 41, where Captain Brian set up shop a couple of decades ago, selling fresh seafood from the Gulf of Mexico. Next came the restaurant which is popular – be prepared for dinnertime line-ups. The menu is primarily seafood, though landlubbers can order beef. Prices are modest – the cheapest entree is fish and chips, lightly breaded scrod with fries and cole slaw – a substantial meal at $6.95, even better with a $3.95 salad bar serving.

Where to stay

Sun-N-Fun, ✪ ($$) ✪ 7125 Fruitville Rd., Sarasota 34240-9729 ✪ 1-800-843-2421 ✪ 941-371-2505 ✪ www.sunnfunfl.com

If the management neglected any detail for a comfortable holiday, we couldn't think of it – except maybe a teapot. Which is surprising since the camp, now 33 years old, is British-owned. Never mind. We brewed tea in a saucepan.

Two miles long and nearly a mile wide, Sun-N-Fun welcomes renters and itinerant RVs. Neat park models, as fully equipped as any small home,

Dean Williams enjoys woodworking, among dozens of hobbies at Sun-N-Fun.

rent by week or month. Golf carts are favoured modes of transport.

Our squeaky clean lair, with a screened lanai running the length of it, overlooked a lake with a lighted fountain. It comprised a bedroom with queen bed and loads of cupboards, a kitchen with full size stove, fridge and every imaginable accessory (except the dratted teapot), and a spacious living room with two comfy couches, each opening to queen size, (extra bedding supplied), separated by a sliding room divider.

With a roof over our heads, we sallied forth to explore the premises. There's an Olympic sized pool heated to 84 degrees, flanked by two bubbling hot tubs. A pleasant all-day snack bar and a restaurant serving a buffet dinner for just $7 pp are adjacent. There's a post office, laundry and hairdresser, billiards, ceramics, lapidary and woodworking studios, computer and fitness rooms. You'll find shuffleboard and a velvet lawn bowling green, an 18-acre spring-fed lake for fishing and non-motor boating, tennis, volleyball.

There are Saturday night dances, square dancing, line dancing, karaoke nights, and on Sundays, inter-denominational church services. During winter months, circus performers from the Gardiner Circus (which often visits Canada) are in residence, practicing trampoline and trapeze acts, much to the delight of residents.

Sales manager Lynn Miller noted that while senior snowbirds push the average age to sixty-plus, she sees increasing numbers of 'junior/seniors' enjoying early retirement or extended winter holidays, and children and grandchildren are much in evidence.

Sun-N-Fun's RV sites rent from about $25; the rental park models range from $240 to $1, 000 per week.

Best Western Golden Host ✪ *4675 N. Tamiami Trail, Sarasota* ✪ *1-800-722-4895* ✪ *941-355-5141* ✪ Handy to all of Sarasota's pleasures, this friendly family operation also has sister Best Western properties, in Venice and in Lakeland. You can expect the usual comfortable but not overly fancy rooms, an expanded continental breakfast, a large pool. What we didn't expect was a spectacular sight at sunset – the vivid green flashes of wild parrots flitting from tree to tree amongst the five acres of swaying palms, colour-drenched hibiscus and other tropical foliage.

Bradenton

Bradenton is a pleasant low-key community strongly committed to environmental and historical restoration. **Old Main Street** comprises a few blocks of nicely preserved vintage shops and office buildings, punctuated by interesting cafes and pubs. *The Lost Kangaroo* ✪ *427 Old Main St.* ✪ *941-747-8114* ✪ is a favourite watering hole.

> **Bradenton Tourist Information: Box 1000, Bradenton, FL 34206**
> ✪ **1-800-822-2017** ✪ **www.flagulfislands.com**

The Village of the Arts ✪ *12th St. W. and 11th Ave. W.* ✪ *www.villageofthearts.com*

Bravo for Bradenton where an exciting redevelopment project is transforming a previously seedy part of town into a charming artists' colony. Thanks to some bylaw changes and street improvements, elderly bungalows are metamorphosing into appealing showplaces for artists to live and sell their work. You can visit anytime – studios post signs if they're open. But during **Art Walk**, the first Friday of each month, 6-9 p.m., the place rocks with studio tours, demonstrations, music and food. The artists are active in community life too, donating art for charities, planning after-school arts programs and participating in downtown events. And plans are afoot for antique shops and outdoor cafes.

The Powel Crosley Museum ✪ *1 Seagate Dr., 8374 North Tamiami Trail, Sarasota* ✪ *941-722-3244*

Powel Crosley was the consummate entrepreneur. He's credited with inventing the first compact car, the electric automobile, the facsimile machine, four-wheel disc brakes and four different airplanes, to name a

Newly renovated South Florida Museum displays prehistoric beasts, Indian artifacts and more.

few. Crosley built a 21-room winter home in Bradenton in 1929, with 10 baths and a three-car carriage house, a swimming pool, yacht basin and seaplane dock. Developers coveted the house but the **Manatee County Commission** rescued it, creating a museum and **'Entrepreneur's Hall of Fame'** in 2000. Still undergoing renovation, the house is open for tours on Wednesdays (call for appointment) and for charity events and holiday showcases several times a year.

South Florida Museum ✪ *201 Tenth St. W., Bradenton, Fla. 34205* ✪ *941-746-4131* ✪ *www.southfloridamuseum.org*

The South Florida Museum displays impressive relics of Florida's near and distant past – a 45-foot alligator, a 20-foot-tall mastodon with four-foot tusks, a six-foot-long armadillo standing four feet high, a shark's jaw twice the height of an average person. A seven-foot tall saber-toothed cat, *(smilodon fatalis)*, both its mighty skeleton and a lifesize mural, looking as menacing as it did 12,000 years ago, greets visitors in the lobby.

But it's a living relic of prehistory that is a favourite. Snooty, aged 54, the oldest manatee bred in captivity, lives in solitary splendour in a huge fresh water tank overlooking the board room. His chief occupation is eating – he devoured 21,800 heads of romaine lettuce last year, plus special treats of monkey chow. The museum is part of a manatee rehabilitation program that nurtures sick or injured manatee and returns them to nature.

But the museum's spectacular scope encompasses much more – Florida's first peoples, the Spaniards, and its showpiece, the Tallant Collection of Florida Indian artifacts, including pottery, and rare gold and silver, bronze and copper artifacts. An ambitious renewal program, now underway, will vastly expand both exhibit space and security for the precious collections.

Mixon Fruit Farms ✿ *2712 26th Ave. E., Bradenton, Fla. 34209-7427* ✿ *1-800-608-2525* ✿ *www.mixon.com*

You may already have tasted Mixon's fresh produce because their fruit is a favourite of Canadian school, church and charity fundraisers. Their 330-acre orchards just east of Bradenton include a huge store where fresh fruit and juice are sold and sampled. Try the orange ripple ice cream made with fresh orange juice, or the calorie-laden fudge. There's also a sandwich bar for quick lunches and shelves of souvenirs.

For Good Sports

If you can't live another minute without ice, strap on your skates and take a spin or join a game. Bradenton boasts three separate hockey rinks with artificial ice so there's year-round hockey, recreational and figure skating.

The J.P. Igloo Ice & Inline Sports Complex ✿ *5309 29th St. E., Ellenton 34222* ✿ *941-723-3663* ✿ *www.jpigloo.com* (I-75, Exit 43) is open 6 am-midnight with two NHL size rinks, a roller rink fitness centre – even a birthday party room. Adm. $6, $3 skate rental. For baseball fans, the **Pittsburgh Pirates'** spring practice sessions in February are free. During March, the 'Grapefruit League' fires up at **McKechnie Stadium, (941-747-3031)** at $6 a ticket.

Ancient Indian mound at Emerson Point Preserve can be visited but not explored.

Bradenton

Silver Resorts on Longboat Key are handy to the beaches and boating of both the Gulf and the Intracoastal Waterway.

Emerson Point Preserve ❂ *Palmetto 34221* ❂ *941-748-4501.*

On an 83-degree March weekday, **Emerson Point Beach** was almost deserted. Two fishermen, up to their belts in the sea, and a groggy chap in a van comprised its entire population. Easy to see why hikers, kayakers and canoers love this area.

Two plants that are threatening Florida's native flora are the Brazilian pepper and Australian pines. Five years ago, county officials declared war and an energetic clearance program is now underway, providing breathing space for native vegetation like lantana and mangroves.

The local government's cultural awareness is also evident in its sensitive handling of an ancient Indian mound, which remains unexcavated until investigative techniques allow researchers to explore the site without desecrating it. Meanwhile, self-guided tours allow visitors to view the area.

The Islands

South of **Tampa Bay**, the Gulf Islands of **Anna Maria** and **Longboat Key** are low-key, low-stress havens, forming a long, skinny expanse of low-rise hotels, motels, houses and small stores with glimpses of the Gulf of Mexico on the west and the Intracoastal Waterway on the east. It's mostly upscale but punctuated with occasional budget places.

Silver Resorts, (www.silverresorts.com), a member of Superior Small Lodgings, offer three beach resorts.

The Silver Sands ✪ 5841 Gulf of Mexico Drive, Longboat Key ✪ ($$) ✪ 1-800-245-3731 ✪ provides 37 one- and two-bedroom apartments and villas, for minimum one-week rentals, starting at about $100 per night. There's a pool, tennis court, putting green and private beach.

The Silver Surf ✪ 1301 Gulf Drive N., Bradenton Beach ✪ ($$) ✪ 1- 800-441-7873 ✪ is a two-story motel-style property with studio suites and apartments, some with screened ocean-front lanais, a private stretch of beach with parasailing and fishing nearby and an easy walk to restaurants. Rates start at $110.

Brand new in 2002 is *Bridgewalk* ✪ ($$$) ✪ 100 Bridge St., Bradenton Beach ✪ 1-866-779-2545. Its 28 huge suites – some as large as 1,700 square feet – open onto spacious screened verandahs from which you can catch Gulf or Waterway views. Handsomely fitted with quality touches such as granite counter tops and Jacuzzi baths, the units can open up to become three or four-bedroom suites for larger families or groups.

Mr. Bones Bar-B-Que ✪ 3007 Gulf Drive, Holmes Beach ✪ 941-778-6614 ✪ Great food and funky décor make this a memorable eatery. It starts with the black wooden coffin just inside the front door where you choose your cold drink and continues to dozens of smiling/snarling primitive masks peering down from every wall. And finally, it's great food – chicken, some vegetarian choices but primarily gigantic servings of BBQ ribs of various flavour persuasions. Thank goodness for a half-size serving, which was still enough for two.

'Choose your poison' from the coffin at Mr. Bones, a funky Bar-B-Que on Holmes Beach, near Bradenton.

St. Pete Beach

The congestion, pollution and crime rates of St. Petersburg, Clearwater and Tampa detract from their undoubtedly fine attractions. St. Pete Beach, a skinny beach-rimmed peninsula, accessible by several causeways, provides a pleasant haven from the madding crowds.

A tiny shopping enclave in St. Pete Beach is **Corey Avenue**, stretching a couple of blocks east from Gulf Blvd. Its highlight is the historic **Beach Theatre**, a fine old movie house still presenting a new movie every week. Shops include an excellent Shell Shop – check out the sand dollar wall clocks – a Christmas shop and for browsers, Suzette's Antiques and Oddities Mall, with a constantly changing roster of . . . well . . . antiques and oddities.

The Don CeSar ✪ *($$$-$$$$)* ✪ *3400 Gulf Blvd., St. Pete Beach, FL 33706* ✪ *1-800-221-0007* ✪ *www.doncesar.com*

The spectacular Don CeSar is a vintage hotel and national historic site, dating from 1928. Not for nothing is it called 'the pink palace'. It sits on **St. Pete Beach** like a vast demented birthday cake with balconies – all pink with frothy white trim, overwrought iron, turrets and towers, colonnades and terraces. This is a very grand hotel and they don't let you forget it – from the stone-faced doormen to the unsmiling receptionists, our welcome wasn't exactly warm. But the hotel has undergone a $2 million

'Pink Palace' of St. Pete Beach is really the historic Don CeSar Hotel. Built in 1928, the hotel recently enjoyed a $2 million facelift.

renovation of late. Inside, it's gleaming and handsomely appointed and its several restaurants are noted for their fine European and 'Floribbean' cuisine. The 277 guest rooms include 50 suites plus 70 one-bedroom condo-style suites at its sister property, the Beach House. The resort levies a $10 per person daily resort fee that covers turn-

Day cruise from Tradewinds Beach stops at Shell Island for high class picking.

down service, shoe shines, in-room safe, parking, daily newspaper, morning coffee in the lobby, and local phone calls.

Lamara Motel ❁ *($-$$)* ❁ *520 73rd Ave., St. Pete Beach, FL 33706*
❁ *1-800-211-5108* ❁ *www.lamara.com*

The north end of St. Pete Beach is strewn with unpretentious motels and seasonal apartments. Amongst them is the **Lamara Motel**, a friendly family establishment, snug behind high fences, already welcoming a substantial Canadian clientele. It's walking distance to shops and affordable restaurants, and an exact 1,550 feet (477 m.) from the beach. (A recent guest, in love with his Christmas GPS, measured it). Various beach bars celebrate each glorious sunset with appropriate libations.

Toronto escapee Steve Kibort, with his wife and daughter, bought the motel in October, 2001. They offer eight efficiencies and eight one-bedroom apartments, some big enough for four or five people. There's a heated swimming pool, a pretty garden, laundry, an outdoor barbecue for guests' use, and a 'take-one, leave-one' book exchange in the main office. To break the ice, there's a potluck barbeque each Wednesday evening, plus a complimentary Sunday pancake breakfast. Lamara is immaculate with well appointed kitchens replete with full sets of dishes and cutlery, new appliances and furnishings. And rentals coddle the budget.

Gardens, patios, waterways abound at the 35-acre Tradewinds, which includes three resorts.

TradeWinds Beach Resorts ✺ ($$$-$$$$), Gulf Boulevard, St. Pete Beach 33706 ✺ 1-800-344-5999 ✺ www.tradwindsresort.com

The 35-acre **TradeWinds** complex right on the beach caters to various price ranges with three adjacent hotels. Check the website for value-priced packages. A $12-per-day flat fee is charged for hotel services such as parking, fitness centre, paddle boats and beach cabanas. An all-points charge card covers17 restaurants and bars, a kids club, and other extras.

The cheapest, the **Sirata Beach Resort**, espouses a Caribbean atmosphere – sunset salutes and steel drums at the bar with free drinks all round and a prize for whoever guesses the exact time of sunset. Most Sirata rooms are 'efficiencies' – meaning a kitchenette, handy for families or anyone on a budget. The westernmost rooms look out to the beach, past a fountain-centred courtyard.

The much grander **Island Grand**, next door, is flanked by lush tropical gardens while an old cracker cottage, removed to this site and floating on pontoons, has been converted to a pool-side bar. The Bermuda Restaurant offers excellent value with its $9.95 breakfast buffet and a comparable early bird (5-6 pm) dinner special .

The upscale **Sandpiper** offers suites with kitchens and bedrooms in a secluded setting.

Capt. Dave's Water Sports ✺ St. Pete Beach ✺ 727-423-4247
✺ www.adventurecruise.net

Captain Ian Henderson is the handsomely bearded barefoot master of a 49-passenger 40-foot catamaran departing from the **TradeWinds Resort** beach. These shelling and snorkel expeditions, usually include bonus close-ups of dolphins and other sea life. A British émigré, Capt. Ian sampled Canada briefly before opting for St. Pete Beach and the boats. This informal cruise puts passengers ashore at **Shell Island** to gather (you guessed it!) shells. **Egmont Key**, with its 1898 fortress built for the Spanish-American War and partially under-water, is an intriguing snorkel site. The half-day trip includes lunch and the use of all required equipment at $50 adults, $35 kids.

For some reason, Capt. Ian Henderson chose Florida over Canada.

P.J.s Seafood Restaurant ✆ *7500 Gulf Blvd. St. Pete Beach* ✆ *727-367-3309 and 500 1st St., Indian Rocks Beach* ✆ *727-596-5898*

We sampled the St. Pete's Beach site but we have it on the best author-ity that P.J.'s second home at Indian Rocks Beach is an exact replica. What you find is a casual, not-too-noisy restaurant serving excellent seafood, from catfish to coconut shrimp to crab, plus pastas, beef and chicken, hearty chowders and generous salads. And a fabulous key lime pie. Entrees average about $13. Hundreds of dollar bills paper the walls, autographed by happy patrons. When redecorating was needed, the bills were removed, making a substantial donation to a local children's hospital.

St. Petersburg

The Pier

Jewly Youschak serves an elegant and copious tea at her St. Petersburg inn.

An inverted pyramid perched beside Tampa Bay, **the Pier** is a happening place. Small souvenir and craft shops plus the kind of food court you'd expect at shopping centres pack the ground floor. The top floor affords a fine view of Tampa Bay. The elegant **Columbia Restaurant** ($$$) on the third floor, founded in 1905, presents a Spanish ambience and Spanish cuisine. The kids will enjoy **Great Explorations**, a hands-on science centre that includes a live snake exhibition and high-class bubble-blowing. (Open Mon-Sat, 10-8, Sun 11-6. Adm: 3-55, $4, 56+, $2, under 3, free.) The second-floor **Tampa Aquarium** provides remarkable views of sea life, some live, some in picture form. We marveled at the brown and white lion fish with fins like butterfly wings; the queen angel fish with iridescent fins floating like feather boas. And we learned that the Black Triggerfish is purple and the harlequin sweet lips has black and white leopard spots. Admission is by donation.

Just out front, pedal-powered surreys are rented, two-seaters, $8 per half hour, four seaters, $10 per half hour.

Inn at the Bay Bed and Breakfast ✪ ($$-$$$) ✪ 126 4th Ave NE, St. Petersburg 33701 ✪ 727-822-1700 ✪ www.innatthebay.com

Just before the Sept. 11, 2001 tragedy, Jewly and Dennis Youschak opened their beautifully renovated inn, a short walk from the **St. Petersburg Pier**. A seedy, rundown hotel, it cost a fortune to gut the place and transform it into an elegant B&B, complete with a top floor honeymoon suite that's worth getting married for and a cobbled yard and quaint gazebo for weddings. After Sept. 11, they had a few quiet months to contemplate their future. But now the rally is underway and their 12 antique-furnished rooms (eight with whirlpool tubs) are filling up.

They've added a splendid tea ($12, noon-4) that begins with your choice of a dozen or so teas, brewed in proper china tea pots. Next comes a mouth-watering three-tier tray of dainties – the mandatory cucumber sandwiches, curried egg sandwiches on croissants, and pesto and pine nut tarts on the first tier; warm lemon scones with Jewly's home-made clotted cream and cranberry jelly on the second; and on the top – and you mustn't touch them until you've finished the other two tiers – the piece de resistance, chocolate dipped strawberries and tiny glasses of cherry cheesecake mousse. The room rate includes a lavish breakfast – fruit, crepes, egg dishes.

The Inn at the Bay offers a 10 per cent discount to Canadians who mention 'Florida, Eh?' when they reserve. (Some blackout periods.)

Safety Harbor Resort and Spa ✪ *($$$)* ✪ *105 North Bayshore Dr., Safety Harbor, FL 34695* ✪ *727-726-1161* ✪ *www.safetyharborspa.com*

Long before Europeans stepped ashore, these mineral springs were esteemed for their curative powers by Indians who lived here for some 12,000 years. In 1944, they opened to visitors as a true 'health spa' and they continue to serve patrons of the upscale **Safety Harbor Resort and Spa**, which offers a wide range of massage and body treatments, plus fitness and nutritional services. There are 193 guest rooms. Various money-saving spa packages are offered (see website).

Inverted pyramid, St. Petersburg Pier is packed with entertaining attractions.

Citrus wines have won 78 awards in five years for Florida Citrus Winery where Gladys and Ray Shook serve samples.

Florida Orange Grove Winery ✪ *1500 Pasadena Ave. S., St. Petersburg* ✪ *1-800-338-7923* ✪ *www.floridawine.com*

There's more to Florida than orange juice. These days, there's award-winning orange wine, along with tangerine, tangelo, grapefruit and key lime, the first citrus wines to be marketed commercially in the state.

The Shook family – parents Gladys and Ray and their son, Vince – took the plunge into citrus wines nearly five years ago, after 10 years of testing and experimentation.

An established citrus operation for nearly three decades, they shipped citrus fruit all over the US and Canada. But the idea of transforming orange juice into wine intrigued them. With the help of a friend, an amateur wine maker who since became an employee, they began their journey into the mysterious world of fermentation, racking, clarifying, stabilizing and bottling. They now produce 21 varieties including novelties such as orange wine fermented with coffee beans and orange/chocolate wine, a Valentine novelty that became so popular that it was added to the year-round list. Vegetables are now on the target – there's a tasty carrot wine, and a tomato wine aged with jalapeno peppers, recommended for spicy meals or for cooking.

In just five years, the Florida Citrus wines have walked off with 78 awards, including five for their most recent key lime wine, a tangy libation reminiscent of margaritas. Open 9 to 5:30 weekdays, 1-5 Sundays.

Duck Tours of Tampa Bay ✪ *Ticket booth at the Pier's front entrance* ✪
727-432-3825 ✪ *www.DuckToursofTampaBay.com*

There's nothing sedate about this land and sea tour of St. Petersburg but if you're in a mood for goofy fun, by all means leap on board. You can't miss **the Duck** – it's an exquisitely ugly vivid yellow World War II DUKW vehicle designed to operate on land or in water. We did both, rumbling along St. Petersburg's classy streets, past historic homes, hotels and high-priced shops,

quacking our duck quackers at pedestrians and chanting "We don't need a trailer" at a startled soul trying to launch his boat. From the streets, we plunged into the ocean, touring the marina to leer at lesser vessels and venturing out into the ocean to play with dolphin, who seem fascinated by this lumbering beast.

Our 80-minute tour was hosted by a guy who called himself Quacker Jack and had a seemingly unlimited store of corny jokes plus plenty of nuggets about the city itself. One such nugget, perhaps an urban legend, concerns a handsome public washroom just off

Have a quacking good time as you steam around St. Petersburg in this WW II vehicle.

the Pier, at Bayshore and Second Avenue. The story goes that a dispute arose between the architect who designed the splendid octagonal St. Mary's Catholic Church a few blocks south, and the church board. Thwarted, he still had the last word, designing a public toilet that reflected the church's design elements. DUCKS offers a comparable tour in Tampa/Ybor City. Adults $18.50, seniors $16.50, kids 3-12 $9.95.

Sponge diving, a major industry in Tarpon Springs 100 years ago, remains a major attraction.

Suncoast Seabird Sanctuary ❂ 18328 Gulf Blvd. Indian Shores 33785 ❂ 727-391-6211 ❂
www.seabirdsanctuary.org

Billed as the largest non-profit wild bird hospital in the U.S., this sanctuary, founded in 1971, is dedicated to 'Rescue, Repair, Recuperation and Release' of sick and injured wild birds. Emergency facilities, a surgical centre, recovery areas and recuperation areas, both indoors and out, nurture some 10,000 birds per year, of which 82 per cent are released. Open 9 to dusk, year-round. Free admission but donations welcome.

Heading North

Dunedin is worth a visit. It's spring training headquarters for the **Toronto Blue Jays** – the local **Holiday Inn** even boasts wall murals in Blue Jays themes.

What's more it's rich in Scottish heritage, which is detailed at the local Historical Museum in the old Orange Belt Railway station. Highland Games each November, a spring Celtic Festival, and regular Friday night Scottish parties, monthly Pipe Band concerts, along with regular injections of Celtic inspiration from its twin cities – **Stirling, Scotland** and **Summerside, PEI** – reinforce Scottish awareness.

The downtown area appeals to walkers with interesting antiques and art galleries, restaurants and several promising B&Bs. At the Arts Centre, a 'Florida Treasures' art mural, a fund-raising work-in-progress by local artists, will on completion contain 3,000 hand-painted glazed ceramic tiles depicting Florida's flora, fauna and history.

Once one of Florida's major seaports, Dunedin prides itself as the birthplace of frozen orange juice concentrate and the WWII amphibious tractor, The Alligator. And the famed A.C. Neilsen ratings, which determine American television tastes, for better or for worse, have originated here since 1972.

Oldsmar was created in 1913 by Ransom Eli Olds, father of the Oldsmobile, dreaming of a lucrative retirement community of 100,000 souls on his newly purchased 37,000 acres. Alas, Mother Nature had other ideas – a hurricane blasted up Tampa Bay and wiped out most of the town. Ten years and some $4.5 million later, Olds moved on, leaving just 200 residents. Today it's quiet and pleasant, but catch it while you can. The population tripled in the 1980s and a new development binge is about to boost the population by nearly 25 per cent.

The population swells each weekend when the *Oldsmar Flea Market (180 Race Track Rd S ☻ 813-855-5306)* fires up. Some 800 vendors line the narrow corridors, selling everything from antique saws to merely old clothes, from plants to carpets, x-rated videos to kids toys, plenty of junk, along with junque and collectibles – it's a paradise for flea market junkies.

Watch for the fantastical pottery creations of **Kris Archodakis**, a retired Greek pilot who crafts smiling ceramic fish and whimsical vases in his Clearwater studio (727-799-2788). Born in Greece, he immigrated to Australia, and then applied for Canadian citizenship. But our all-wise immigration department turned him down so he applied to the US and was immediately accepted. You'll find Kris in his Greek fisherman's cap in a corner booth in Building A at Bridge Line.

At Oldsmar's vast flea market, ceramic artist Kris Archodakis smiles back at his droll fish.

Tarpon Springs

Tarpon Springs is a memory of Greece transplanted to Florida's west coast. Sponge diving was a major industry a century ago and still this city's chief attraction. Greek sponge divers came to Tarpon Springs in 1905 and built the world's largest sponge industry. By the mid-30s, 200 boats were harvesting some $3 million worth of sponges a year. Then disaster struck – a bacterial blight that killed the sponges and along with them, most of the industry. The old Sponge Exchange is now a shopping and dining enclave awash in Greek foods and handicrafts. The elder statesman of the Tarpon sponge industry is George Billiris whose vintage 1920s *Sponge Warehouse (26 W. Park St* ✆ *727-938-0787)*, listed in the National Register of Historic Places, sells sponges worldwide.

The St. Nicholas Boat Line (693 Dodecanese Blvd. ✆ *727-942-6425)* offers 35-minute cruises that explain the history of sponge diving. (Adults $5, kids $1).

St. Nicholas Greek Orthodox Church in Tarpon Springs is an extravagant neo-Byzantine structure, modeled after St. Sophia in Istanbul, its lofty interior lighted by fine stained glass windows and decorated with elaborate icons and Grecian marble. An émigré from Canada, Nicholas Peppas, joined the Greek migration to Tarpon Springs in 1907 and spearheaded fund-raising for the first church, which was replaced in the 30s by the present building, funded by donations from local sponge fishermen.

Tarpon Springs' splendid St. Nicholas Greek Orthodox Church was funded by donations from sponge fishermen.

The wilderness of north central Florida has many faces and many names. They call it **'the real Florida'** or **'the hidden Florida'** and it's both of those. Maybe 'the forgotten Florida' applies – tourism has passed it by, leaving a world of wilderness, rivers, coastlines and tiny villages, all waiting to be discovered. Substantial chunks of this area are reserved as parks and refuges, raising hopes that for future generations, **the 'Original Florida'** – its most recent moniker – will retain its untrammeled beauty.

Around the 'big bend' and south from the **Panhandle's** white powder beaches, the landscape gives way to dense wood-

Unspoiled wilderness of north-central Florida supports hiking, camping, kayaking, canoeing.

lands, criss-crossed by broad rivers that are fed by hundreds of powerful springs. The coastline is wilder here and some of the salt marshes stretch inland for miles. Along the shoreline from **St. Mark's River** below **Tallahassee**, past **Steinhatchee** to **Suwanee**, you can sea kayak the **Big Bend Saltwater Paddling Trail**, the state's first designated water trail, camping on isolated beaches as you go.

Fishing is both pastime and business on this coast. The shallow waters of **Apalachee Bay** make for excellent fishing year-round. During the July to early September season, scallops are so plentiful that you can scoop them up off the sandy ocean floor. The villages of **Keaton Beach** and **Steinhatchee** are well equipped with marinas, sport fishing facilities and fishing camps as well as local experts who know where to fish and how to land the big ones.

Big one that didn't get away is typical catch for fishing guide Pat McGriff of Keaton Beach.

Inland, near the I-75, there are larger centers – **Alachua, High Springs** and **Gainesville**, where the University of Florida maintains a prestigious presence.

The little old fishing village of Steinhatchee nestles on the shore where the Steinhatchee River flows into the Gulf. Until recently, it had nothing much to recommend it except fishing and freedom. Today, tourism is thriving, largely thanks to the leadership of **Dean Fowler** whose upscale **Steinhatchee Landing Resort**, backed by progressive marketing skills that he shares with local and state tourism councils, has set a new standard. A town on the move, Steinhatchee is emerging as an excellent base from which to explore of the whole area.

Steinhatchee Landing Resort ✪ ($$-$$$) ✪ Box 789, Steinhatchee, FL 32359 ✪ (Hwy. 51, off Hwy. 19, west of Gainesville) ✪ 352-498-3513 ✪ 1-800-584-1709 ✪ www.steinhatcheelanding.com

Three miles upstream from the Gulf of Mexico on the Steinhatchee River, Dean Fowler built a dream village. A hands-on creative dynamo, Dean wasn't ready to retire when he sold his chain of nursing homes so he set to work to reproduce a 19th century 'cracker' village.

Cracker houses, so-called for the whip cracking of Florida's early cowboys, are a distinctive style – raised on stilts to let air circulate underneath, with airy screened porches and plenty of windows to enhance cross-ventilation. Rocking chairs are mandatory accessories. Dean Fowler's cracker houses differ somewhat from the original though, thanks to air conditioning, indoor plumbing and modern kitchens. Several have main-floor bedrooms for ease of mobility. Fully equipped kitchen, dining and lounge areas are upstairs. These days, 30 pastel-toned houses nestle amid mature trees with winding paths, flowers and the broad gentle river nearby.

Former US president Jimmy Carter recognized the resort's appeal. He brought his entire family there (19 Carters, 13 secret service agents) for a family reunion, to revel in old-fashioned activities like canoeing, bonfires and marshmallow roasts.

Time seems to stand still at the resort, but Dean Fowler does not. He's constantly adding new features and facilities such as the petting zoo with its flock of ultra-friendly goats. The goat barn is constructed of antique lumber salvaged from a Georgia plantation house that began life around 1836 as a railroad hotel.

The newest developments are a wedding chapel and eight luxurious honeymoon cottages. (See also 'Weddings' page 180). Equipped with every possible amenity, the cottages have spacious living/dining areas with 32-in. TVs, and glass-enclosed gas fireplaces visible from both living room and bathroom. Fully equipped kitchens include dishwashers and stacking washer/dryers. The bathrooms have oversize spa tubs, cushy bathrobes and deluxe bath products. A wedding party could occupy the entire resort, since the convention centre is as suitable for wedding receptions as it is for corporate events.

The temptation to sit on the porch and let the world go by would be irresistible if it weren't for the lure of the river, and the mighty wilderness of ocean, forests and powerful springs within easy reach. The Resort rents both canoes and bicycles and in the nearby town, boats are available for sport fishing.

Cracker-style cottages with all amenites ensure relaxation at Steinhatchee Landing.

The Steinhatchee River Inn ✪ ($$) ✪ 352-498-4049 ✪ half a mile down the road, joined the group after extensive renovations in 1993. It offers a budget-conscious alternative to the Resort, with 17 suites, some with kitchens, a swimming pool and picnic tables.

Steinhatchee

A sleepy fishing village, Steinhatchee retains its rustic charm while attracting fisherfolk with good services, food and lodging options.

Steinhatchee was a sleepy fishing village until Dean Fowler arrived. It's still a fishing village but thanks to his energy and leadership – he served on the board of **'the Original Florida'**, which represents 11 counties of North Central Florida, and now the board of directors of **Visit Florida**, which markets the state worldwide – the entire area is fast emerging as a peaceful vacation destination that weds wilderness to history, good lodging and fine food.

Pets are welcome at Steinhatchee if they weigh less than 28 pounds and promise to be nice to Justin, Dean's snow-white Maltese. For pets, a security deposit and pre-checkout inspection are required.

Sea Hag Marina, ✪ *($$)* ✪ *322 Riverside Drive, Steinhatchee* ✪ *352-498-3008* ✪ *www.seahag.com* ✪ is a busy marina offering all kinds of fishing and boating gear from its large ships' store, bait and tackle, boat storage, marine mechanics and fishing expeditions with the best charter captains in the area. They also rent a two-bedroom smartly remodeled apartment, above the store, a one-bedroom motor home and a rustic riverfront room with a deck, complete with whirlpool, over the river.

Wood's Gulf Breeze Marina & Campground, Steinhatchee ✪ *($-$$)* ✪*352-498-3948* ✪ is a large marina and campground at the mouth of the Steinhatchee River. Besides boat rentals and charters, Wood's offers accommodation – from tent camping to oversize RVs with tows, plus furnished houses and mobile homes, and a five-bedroom house.

Canadian bargains

Dollars at Par

Steinhatchee Landing Resort continues its policy of accepting Canadian dollars at par during winter months, except major US holiday periods. Payment in Canadian dollars is preferred, rather than credit cards. The offer extends only to accommodations and some restrictions and blackouts apply. **Call for details: 1-800-584-1709.**

Sunset Place Condo Motel ✪ *($$)* ✪ *115 First St. SW, Steinhatchee* ✪ *1-877-860-0860* ✪ *352-498-0860* ✪ *www.sunsetpl.com* ✪ is a long blue and white building with a spectacular view of the bay from its spacious unscreened balconies. One and two-bedroom apartments – the larger units have a spiral staircase to an upper loft – are smartly furnished with big kitchens. There's a large pool.

Fiddler's Restaurant ✪ *($-$$)* ✪ *1306 SE Riverside Dr., Steinhatchee* ✪ *352-498-7427* ✪ *www.steinhatchee.com/restaurants*

There's nothing pretentious about this comfortable restaurant at Steinhatchee's waterfront – just high quality seafood, carefully prepared and a super warm welcome from the Hunt family, Jim, Joyce, Jared and Jill, who make it all happen.

Big genial Jim Hunt is the chef and a picky one too, a stickler for fresh seafood and fresh veggies, conscious of low-sodium, low-fat diets, kind to vegetarians. Since this is fishing territory, the menu is understandably heavy on seafood – lots of shrimps, scallops, grouper, flounder and combo plates – but land-lubbers can nosh on steak, chicken or ribs, all modestly priced. Save room for the key lime cheesecake or brownies with ice cream.

Open year-round, Wed-Sun, 11-10; July 1-Sept 10 (scallop season), seven days a week.

Pelican Point Inn ✪ *($$)* ✪ *352-498-7427* ✪ is a recent Hunt family initiative next to the restaurant. Its 18 rooms include two suites, plus three-person and two-person rooms. All rooms have refrigerators, microwaves and screened back porches and rates include continental breakfast.

The Road to Nowhere

Dean Fowler of **Steinhatchee Landing Resort** has acquainted himself with all the hidden places around the countryside. For example, near **Jena**, south of Steinhatchee Village, two nearly invisible roads lead off from Highway 361 toward the sea, recalling a 1970s era of drug smugglers and crooked politicians.

A well-paved highway, straight as an arrow, slices through untouched wilderness. Not a house, not even a shack is visible. Civilization is far away. And for good reason. This is the **'Road to Nowhere'**, which was built at taxpayers' expense three decades ago, as a landing strip for airborne drug smugglers. To facilitate the nighttime landings, the smugglers parked a car at each end of the 'strip' so the lights could serve as a guide. Nonetheless at least one plane crashed, killing one of its occupants and bringing the feds down on a drug ring that had been operating for years while local authorities turned blind eyes. In fact, the smugglers got themselves elected to local government so they could build their airstrip and continue their operations without irritating interference. Several of them served jail sentences. Many more filled their bank accounts and were never brought to justice. It's a story that most locals would rather not discuss but the 'Road to Nowhere' remains as a well paved testimony to the scheme.

That road leads toward the sea through thousands of acres of sand flats, green in summer, black with sawgrass in winter. Limestone boulders, their tops smoothed by years of battering from high tides, poke above the sand. Small hammocks of elevated land support sudden bursts of tall growth – live oaks, cedars and pine, fragrant myrtle, cabbage palms and palmettos, all happily co-existing within a landscape just a few inches higher than the salt flats. You can hike for miles, or launch a boat or canoe in Cow Creek, which

Near the 'Road to Nowhere', salt marshes stretch for miles, broken by boulders and tiny islands of foliage.

Running the rapids at Steinhatchee Falls, Montrealer Annabelle Chvostek samples canoeing opportunities in 'the original Florida.'

local fishermen use to reach the sea.

Only five miles further north, Dean showed us a dramatically different landscape. **Sink Creek Road** also points toward the sea but in place of salt marshes there is a towering forest – great twisting live oaks whose green leaves last all winter, pine, cedar, native red-berried holly, and a bush called ilex vomitaria, used by native people to induce vomiting.

Yet another wilderness is revealed just north-east of Steinhatchee, near the intersection of Hwy. 51 and 19, where an unmarked gravel road enters a dense tangle of trees, shrubs and palmettos. A narrow path, probably first used by Indians and later by fishermen hauling their boats across country, cuts through heavy woods beside what looks like a small creek. It's actually the **Steinhatchee River**, newly emerged from underground, flowing through a deep steep-sided chasm, sometimes dropping out of sight again only to emerge a little further along, floating with exquisite yellow water lilies, disappearing again to emerge further on, bubbling out of a rocky cave, dropping out of sight and popping u p as a lovely little lake. The terrain is rough with deep brief valleys, steep hillocks and water-filled caves, for here the river, flowing underground and partnered with heavy rains, has weakened the limestone surface causing sink holes and caves. Small holes, just a foot or two across, hint at deep dark water far below. Here fishermen plant their folding chairs and bait their hooks with chicken livers to catch black catfish that dwell in caverns. Dean Fowler calls it ice-fishing.

Steinhatchee

Steinhatchee Outpost

Steinhatchee Outpost ✪ ($) ✪ 1-800-589-1541 ✪ www.steinhatcheeout-post.com

If you'd like to experience north-central Florida in the raw, you should meet Bishop Clark. In that part of the world, everybody knows him as Bish – a genial giant of a guy, big in both stature and vision.

Bish runs his family's gas station business – it has been operating since 1917. These days, along with gas bars, there are convenience stores, camps for hunters and fishers and an RV park next to his Chevron station at Hwys. 52 and 19.

Lately he expanded again to include wilderness cabins, out in the middle of nowhere – rustic places that appeal to ardent birdwatchers, or to artists, photographers or writers in search of isolation and inspiration. Talk about **'original Florida'** – one of his cabins, 'way out in sawgrass country, has a pump for water. Others have electricity and running water but no TV or phones. Furnishings are sparse. On one property on the Steinhatchee River you can even find shards of pottery, the legacy of Indians who lived there 10,000 years ago. So far Bish has collected four parcels of land, each with a cabin or house, and he'll add more whenever opportunity and dollars are available.
Rental rates are on his website.

His idea is to create hiking and biking trails that give visitors access to the huge state-owned parcel of land once exploited by Proctor and Gamble for pulp and paper. Its potential for eco-travel is awesome.

One of the prettiest canoe routes was the tree-draped Steinhatchee River, quiet and gentle, except at **Steinhatchee Falls**, a brief but turbulent white water section, more a mini-rapid than a waterfall.

The wildlife here is amazing. Canoeing and hiking these byways, we saw plenty of fish and sea birds, and we met owls and turtles practically face to face. Ospreys nest in the bald cypress trees and alligators lurk just at the water's surface.

Bish Clark is champion of Steinhatchee area wilderness

Running the rapids at Steinhatchee Falls, Bish Clark guides Canadian visitors, Alyson Vishnovska (front) and Annabelle Chvostek.

Bish is a fourth generation Floridian. He grew up around here – Keaton Beach, Perry, Steinhatchee – and as a kid, he hunted and fished here. He's as at-home in a boat as on land. He has rattling good tales to tell of fishing expeditions and encounters with sharks and he swears they're true. He shares some of them on his website – check them out.

Bish was probably an environmentalist long before the term was invented. The desecration of land and sea troubles him – he has pulled tons of trash out of the landscape. And he steadfastly refuses to rent his cabins to anyone who fails to respect the environment. On a broader scale, he is actively pushing for conservation of the wilderness, and for ways to share it without destroying it.

He could use some help. In fact, he's looking for handypersons who will swap a few months of their skills in carpentry, plumbing and electrical work for housing, helping to transform his undeveloped properties into slightly less rustic lodgings.

Annabelle Chvostek and Alyson Vishnovska
Annabelle and Alyson are Montreal artists and wilderness enthusiasts.

Staff at Deal's Oyster House beat out the rhythm on the peasle tree.

Deal's Famous Oyster House ✪ ($-$$) ✪ *Hwy 98 West, Perry* ✪ 904-584-4966 This venerable establishment, about 20 miles (32 km) north of Steinhatchee, has been purveying oysters and other seafood for nearly four decades. Oysters are shucked as you watch and served up on the half shell – by the bushel if that's your fancy – or steamed or fried and sometimes served with shrimps or mullet. Along with them come hush puppies – little deep-fried nuggets of something related to grits, slaw or salad and the inevitable French fries. We tried swamp cabbage, its mild sweet flavour reminiscent of both cabbage and turnip. The restaurant, now under the new management of Margaret Seago, serves no alcohol and accepts no credit cards.

But there's entertainment. Years ago, an itinerant performer stopped by, bearing a strange musical contraption that caught owner Roy Deal's eye and ear. It's called a **peasle tree** and it resembles a pogo stick with add-ons – a brass cymbal at the top, further down a drum and tambourine and an enthusiastic staffer who carries it from table to table, shaking thumping and rapping the contraption with a drumstick to add cacophonous rhythm to fast-paced music such as 'Down Yonder'.

Alachua County and its immediate environs are richly endowed with little-known treasures and friendly folks.

So screech to a halt round I-75's Exit 399, (prev. #78) and check it out. You can expect dozens of fresh water springs, pumping millions of gallons of crystal clear water up from the aquifer for the delight of swimmers, snorkelers and divers. Four mighty rivers – the **Steinhatchee**, the **Itchetucknee**, the **Sante Fe** and the **Suwanee** (immortalized by songwriter **Stephen Foster** who never laid eyes on it) roll toward the sea, inviting canoeing and tubing.

Tiny **High Springs**, just five miles (8 km) from the I-75, is a veritable hotbed of creative and eccentric people, intent on maintaining a quality lifestyle that honours the past and nurtures the environment.

Surrounded by natural wonders – massive forests, broad rivers, gargantuan springs – this delightful town of some 3,500 souls has become a respite from the rat race for artists, artisans, antique dealers and anyone seeking a gentler way of life.

Main Street is lined with interesting shops and restaurants in historic buildings. But be prepared for interesting liquor laws. On Sundays, restaurants cannot open their bars but you can bring your own beer or wine. And theatre – there's the **High Springs Community Theater**, run by volunteers, the **Priest Theater**, built in 1926 for minstrel shows and now showing movies Friday to Monday, and the **Theater of Memory**, upstairs at a neat shop and health-conscious café, **The Great Outdoors**.

Retirement Home for Horses, Box 2100, Alachua FL 32616-2100. (County Road 235A, I-75 Exit 399, prev. 78) ✪ *386-462-1001* ✪ *www.millcreekfarm.org*

Sick, abused, neglected or merely old, the horses who arrive at **Mill Creek Farm**, the **Retirement Home for Horses**, are usually near death's door. Peter and Mary Gregory provide day-round, year-round care - enriched diets, veterinarian visits and best of all 245 acres of rolling meadows and trees. The British-born couple, now seniors, created a charity, donated their farm to it and took a vow of poverty to ensure the farm's continuance. And they work like . . . well . . . horses. Seven days a week, year-round, no holidays.

The Farm deals with all sorts of equine disabilities – elderly horses no longer fit for their police, circus or carriage duties; toothless horses who, in lieu of grass, need a soft mash five times daily; blind horses or those suffering from emphysema, kidney disease, liver disease or wounds from abuse or accidents.

They arrive emaciated, lame, sick, scared. One shipment brought eight bags of bones, rescued from a southern Florida farm. Grazing in green pastures, fed vitamin supplements, groomed and nurtured, they soon looked plump and glossy. It's startling to compare this contented herd to the skeletal wrecks revealed by arrival photos.

Zipping about in a golf cart, Peter visits every pasture several times daily, hauling hay and buckets of special feed and checking for problems – lameness, cuts, signs of illness.

The farm loses about one horse a month, each one a personal loss to its caregivers. But for each horse that dies, a live oak is planted on the property, ensuring shade and protection for horses and wildlife for centuries to come.

The farm receives no government or SPCA money. Visitors – and that includes Canadians – can sponsor a horse at $40 per month.

Volunteers are welcome too. Our Toronto Star article about the farm inspired teachers **Ron Ritchie** and **Wendy Case** of **Seaforth District High School in Seaforth, Ontario** to give their 'Bridges to Agriculture' students a unique experience. Eight of them volunteered for a week-long stint at Mill Creek Farm, installing miles of board fencing, clearing brush, feeding and caring for the horses, pressure washing and painting the barn and winning the heartfelt appreciation of Peter and Mary Gregory, who know all about hard work and its rewards.

Mill Creek Farm is open Saturdays only, 11-3 pm. Admission is two carrots, an entire bag is better and cash donations are welcomed.

Marjorie Kinnan Rawlings Homestead, Cross Creek, off Rte. 325 ☼ *352/466-3672*

Author Marjorie Kinnan Rawlings was an intrepid woman. A journalist from the north, she moved with her husband to the raw wilderness of Alachua County in 1928. Her husband left but Rawlings stayed on, managing the 72-acre citrus farm, and writing Pulitzer Prize-winning books – The Yearling, South Moon Under, When the Whippoorwill, Cross

Peter Gregory has devoted his life to caring for injured and abused horses at his Alachua farm.

Marjorie Kinnan Rawlings prepared gourmet meals in her rustic kitchen and pantry.

Creek, and many more. Rawlings believed that cooking was as fine an art as writing and she practiced both, even producing a cookbook called Cross Creek Cookery and entertaining some of the great names of her time – **F. Scott Fitzgerald, Ernest Hemingway** and **Tom Wolfe** among them – whose autographed books fill the shelves.

Her homestead, now a state historic site, includes her nicely preserved cracker-style house. The screened porch was her writing studio – her manual typewriter and a manuscript remain there. She had the first bathroom in the area, a claw-foot tub and toilet purchased from Sears-Roebuck. She installed a generator for electric lighting and to achieve a gentler effect in her living room, she covered the bulbs with chandeliers made from painted wooden butter bowls.

Guided tours that capture Rawlings' wit, courage and creativity are offered Thursday through Sunday at 10, 11, 1, 2, 3 and 4. Only 10 people are admitted at one time so be prepared for a walk in the pleasant citrus orchard Adm: $3.

Santa Fe Canoe Outpost, Box 592, High Springs, FL. 32643 (Hwy 441 from I75, at Santa Fe River Bridge) ☎ *386-454-2050* ☎ *www.santaferiver.com*

There are myriad ways to enjoy Florida's rivers – swimming, snorkeling, diving, fishing. But Jim Wood, who escaped to Florida from a high-powered sales position in Philadelphia a decade ago, knows the best way – the laid-back serenity of a gentle canoe ride.

Jim and his wife, Sally, abandoned the rat race to move to High Springs where they operate the **Santa Fe Canoe Outpost**. You can rent canoes and all the trimmings – from tents to toilet paper – or join Jim Wood on one of his canoe expeditions on the Santa Fe, Ichetucknee or Suwanee Rivers, meandering through wilderness that seems never to have seen mankind. Along the Santa Fe, a two-hour canoe ride showed us elderly cypress trees ringed by knobby 'cypress knees', the outcroppings by which they reproduce. We saw herons and ibis, egrets and ducks. Dozens of turtles – yellow-bellied sliders with (you guessed it) yellow bellies – sunned themselves. An alligator, imitating a log, floated past.

That day, our destination was **Poe Springs**, one of Florida's little known treasures. Set within a 202-acre park, it's one of Alachua County's largest springs, producing some 45 million gallons each day. This nearly deserted park is operated jointly by Alachua County and the YMCA of Gainesville.

One of Jim Woods' innovations is a full moon canoe ride, held on the Saturday nearest the full moon. This five-mile guided expedition, usually 20 or more canoes, leaves after sunset, wending its way between heavily wooded banks, to **Lily Springs** where caretaker/storyteller Ed Watts spins tall tales before a blazing bonfire, complete with hot dogs and marshmallows. Then it's back to the river, a bit more paddling, and a van ride back to home base. Full moon tours cost $20 per person. Reservations are a must.

A two-bedroom cabin with dining area, kitchen and bath, costing $65 per person is offered at the Outpost's headquarters.

Ginnie Springs Outdoors ❂ *7300 NE Ginnie Springs Rd., High Springs, FL 32643* ❂ *386 - 454-7188* ❂ *www.ginniespringsoutdoors.com*

Nature's incredible gift to Florida is its fresh-water springs – hundreds of them – pumping millions of gallons of crystal clear water into lakes and rivers, for the pleasure of swimmers, divers and tubers.

Loaded for fun, tubers arrive at Ginnie Springs for a floating good time.

Ginnie Springs, a family-owned recreation park near High Springs, set within 200 acres of wooded wilderness, is endowed with seven springs, the largest pumping 30 million gallons a day. The water, 21 deg. C (72 F) year-round, flows into the

Sante Fe River which at six degrees warmer than the springs, delights paddlers and tubers. For certified cave divers there's a complex of underwater caves. Divers at all levels, from basic to advanced, can obtain expert instruction. Campsites, both wilderness and serviced, pull-through RV sites and a cottage that sleeps up to eight people are all available – or you can just go and play for a day.

For certified divers, there are interesting challenges. The spring pool drops about 15 feet where large boulders mark the entrance to a cavern that's over six feet high and 20 feet wide. Beyond that room, and past a limestone breakdown, you enter the "ballroom" – 30 feet high and perhaps 70 feet wide with a solid sand floor. Steel bars restrict unsafe areas of the cavern and guidelines lead back to the entrance, for safety's sake.

Excellent diving, including cave diving and instruction, are Ginnie Springs Outdoors specialties.

Diving and tubing gear is available at the **Ginnie Springs** store and there's a pleasant snack bar on site.

Grady House Bed & Breakfast ❂ 420 NW 1st Avenue (Box 205), High Springs, FL 32655 ❂ 386 454-2206 ❂ www.gradyhouse.com

Imagine a room with 350 nudes! Pictures, that is. You'll find it at the **Grady House** in **High Springs**. This interesting house, built in the late

1800s, served as the town's first bakery, later a boarding house for railroad workers. Today it's an award-winning bed and breakfast, plus a complete house next door.

Owners Tony Boothby and Kirk Eppenstein have five rooms, each with private parlour and bath, lovingly furnished with period furniture and accessories. Their huge garden, shaded by tall trees and shrubbery, is accented by statuary and pools, a secluded gazebo complete with hammock and overhead fan and tables for al fresco breakfasts.

And about those nudes? They are paintings, photographs, advertisements and pamphlets of every persuasion and era, an amusing and interesting accent in a remarkable house.

A sampling of the 350 nudes that strut their stuff at Grady House B&B, once High Springs' bakery.

Next door is century-old **Skeet's Cottage** – two bedrooms upstairs, parlour, kitchen and bath downstairs. The house is filled with historic photos documenting the life of **Juanita 'Skeet' Easterlin**, a strong-willed woman, openly lesbian, who served time both as mayor of High Springs and (in penitentiary) for running moonshine, taking the rap for other prominent townspeople who accorded her a ticker tape parade on her triumphant return from the clink. Skeet's ashes, and the bodies of some of her 35 cats, are buried in the garden. Grady House rates range from $90 to $115. Skeet's Cottage costs $185 per night, $725 per week. All rates include an outstanding full breakfast.

The Panhandle
Swap Snow for Snowy Beaches

From Apalachicola to the Alabama border, there's a swath of Florida that's 'unknown' except to flocks of Canadians who migrate there each winter. We suspect they swear an oath of secrecy to avoid attracting tourist hordes to the Panhandle's sugar-fine beaches and tranquil villages. Besides, Canada's coldest months are also off-season for most of the Panhandle so accommodation prices plummet up to 50 per cent.

Wakulla Springs State Park ❂ *550 Wakulla Park Drive, Wakulla Springs* ❂ *850-224-5950* ❂ *www.myflorida.com* ❂ sits at the apex of the 'big bend' where the Florida peninsula segues into the Panhandle. At the heart of this 2,860-acre wildlife sanctuary, the grand-daddy of springs, one of the largest in the world, blasts a billion gallons of crystal clear water up into the Wakulla River every day. If you're nervy, you can leap from the lofty observation tower into the three-acre bowl of the spring. Calmer folk opt for the glass-bottom boat ride over the spring, although the informative commentary is frequently inaudible, thanks to sound systems modeled after those in bus stations.

Wakulla in Seminole means 'strange and mysterious waters' and these are just that. The skeleton of a mastodon has been hauled from the spring and in the vast underwater caverns, only recently explored, fossilized bones of giant sloth, armadillos, camels and other prehistoric animals remain. Several **Tarzan** movies were shot here in the forties. Birds love the place – herons, egrets, bald eagles, ospreys, vultures and anhinga are among the 180 species that hang out here, along with many migrating birds. The park stages a 'Welcome Back Songbirds' festival in late April.

Wakulla Springs Lodge ($$) ❂ *850-224-5950* ❂ is a grand old place, all marble and wrought iron and carved wood. The splendid lobby has an impressive 13-foot ceiling, intricately painted. In a display case sits 'Old Joe', a giant 'gator that lived in the river. He was perhaps 200 years old,

Nine little turtles all in a row sun themselves on a quiet log in the watery wilderness of northwest Florida.

Grand old Wakulla Springs Lodge boasts an intricately painted 13-foot ceiling in the lobby.

11 feet long and 650 pounds, when he was killed in 1966. There's a dining room, snack bar and 27 guest rooms, with surprisingly modest rates, and a single TV set, in the lobby.

Further west, **Apalachicola** is a handsome and historic waterfront city. Its palm-lined streets and beautiful old buildings recall the early 1800s glory days when the city was a thriving port shipping cotton to Europe and New England. Apalachicola has another claim to fame – air conditioning – invented in the mid-1800s by a young doctor named John Gorrie to enhance the comfort of his yellow fever patients. These days, the major industry is seafood – especially oysters, crabs, shrimp and fish.

The Consulate ❂ (*$$*) ❂ *Water Street, Apalachicola* ❂ *1-800-624-3964* ❂ *www.florida-beach.com* ❂ comprises four one- and two-bedroom suites, ranging from 600 to 1,650 square feet, with modern kitchens and handsome furnishings. The location is the historic Grady Building, which housed the French consulate in the early part of the 20th century.

St. George Island State Park ❂ *1900 E. Gulf Beach Dr., St. George Island* ❂ *850-927-2111* ❂ is another skinny barrier island, linked to the mainland by a six-mile causeway from **Apalachicola**. The park access road is lined with monster houses, appearing even bigger because they're hoisted on stilts in accordance with anti-hurricane building codes. Like contemporary castles, many rise three or four stories topped by a look-out tower, providing the owners, but not the passing hoi-polloi, with an uninterrupted view of the sea.

The park itself is treed with pine and ringed by nine miles of sand dunes and beaches, with myriad shells and sand so fine that it squeaks when you walk on it. Pottery shards, relics of native visitors some 5,000 years ago, can still be found. The beaches are rarely crowded, except for the shorebirds – snowy plovers, least terns, black skimmers and willets – that hang out here.

St. George Inn ✪ *($-$$)* ✪ *135 Franklin Blvd., St. George Island* ✪ *1-800-332-5196* ✪ *www.stgeorgeisland.com* ✪ is a handsome edifice just a few yards from the causeway. Recently renovated, it offers one- and two-bedroom suites with views of both beach and bay, and third-floor suites with private balconies for sunrise/sunset views. Wrap-around verandahs with rockers, a large pool and landscaped gardens add to the ambience. Continental breakfast is included; restaurants are within walking distance.

A blue heron waits hopefully for a stray bit of bait as a young boy fishes at St. Joe's.

Just sand dunes, beach and sea await at St. Joe's Beach,
named the top beach in North America.

St. Joseph Peninsula State Park ✿ *8899 Cape San Blas Rd., Port St.
Joe, 32456* ✿ *850-227-1327*

St. Joseph Peninsula spears the ocean like a sandy needle, off the
Panhandle coast. It's one of the loveliest places in Florida with miles and
miles of snowy beaches stretching along either shore, just a few hundred
metres apart. In fact St. Joe's was recently named the best beach in the
U.S. in the 'Dr. Beach' annual ratings.

Handsome park cabins with AC and electricity, with names like Flounder
and Scallop, Porpoise and Starfish, hide amongst the trees overlooking
the sea. Beneath tall pines and palms are campsites, serviced RV and
trailer sites. Millions of shells litter the beach, free for the picking. (You
must not collect live shells). Boardwalks protect the fragile sand dunes.
There's a boat ramp, change rooms, toilets, picnic tables.

Birdlife is plentiful here and we saw three pretty dear grazing by the
roadside. In a fresh water pond, an alligator swam lazily.

A sea of realtor signs, unloading the high-end houses that have sprout-
ed like weeds along either edge of the peninsula, dominates the
approach to the park, along Cape San Blas Blvd., off Hwy. 30A.
Fortunately the scenery improves once you're inside.

The Entrance, 8048 Cape San Blas Road - Port St. Joe, FL 32456 ✿ *St.
Joe's Park entrance* ✿ *850-227-7529* ✿ *www.escapetothecape.com* ✿

The Entrance is a store and then some at the gateway to **St. Joe's Park**.
It's packed with every conceivable vacation need from bathing suits to

boat rentals, from beach umbrellas to bait, from books to beer, from sunscreen to seafood. This is one of the few places offering horseback riding on the beach and you can rent Ringo, Beemer, Presidio or Comanche for an hour or a day. Two skilled horsewomen/guides accompany each ride, match horse to rider and offer safety helmets. An acceptable horse gratuity is a carrot or two. (Reservations recommended).

Co-owner Julia Cunningham is a go-getter and major booster for her area. She recently convinced the local and state powers-that-be to fund a new bike path, to the tune of $700,000. It will start at the St. Joseph State Park, and run the whole length of Cape San Blas Road, nearly nine miles, with completion slated for 2005.

Down to the sea on horseback -- riding is another option for enjoying the beaches at St. Joseph's State Park.

The Turtle Beach Inn ❂ *140 Painted Pony Rd., Port St. Joe.* ❂ *850-229-9366* ❂ *www.turtlebeachinn.com*

This recently opened B&B has four ocean-view rooms and a two-bedroom cottage. The Inn also manages rentals of privately owned homes nearby so there's a broad range of accommodations. Rates range from $90 to $200 per night.

St. Vincent's National Wildlife Refuge occupies a nine-mile island, accessible only by boat, west of St. George Island. It's home to many endangered and threatened species as well as some exotic animals, introduced during its years as a private hunting preserve. Among them is a herd of sambar deer, an elk native to southeast Asia. They weigh in at 500 to 600 pounds but peacefully share the island with the svelt 100-

A pretty dear grazes by the roadside in St. Joseph's Park, not too nervous of passing motorists.

pound native white-tailed deer. Bald eagles nest here, loggerhead turtles find sanctuary and endangered red wolves are bred here to help restore wolf populations in parks further north.

No motorized vehicles are permitted on the island.

The St Vincent Island Shuttle ✪ *850-229-1065* ✪ offers daily year-round service ($10 adult round trip, $7 for kids under 10) from Indian Pass Road in Port St. Joe. Call ahead for schedule. The company also offers guided walking tours of the island and rents bikes ($25 for shuttle, rental and transport) or take your own ($20 for shuttle and transport). Another option is a cruise that puts you ashore at various points of interest around the island and allows you to see the protected shorebird nesting area, not accessible by foot.

The same company offers fishing expeditions aboard their 24-foot pontoon craft, especially appealing to families with children. Depending upon the season, the catch might be tarpon, redfish, Spanish mackerel or trout. The 2.5-hour trips cost $25 pp, minimum four.

St. Joe Wildlife Sanctuary and Education Center ✪ *Port St. Joe* ✪ *850-229-9464* ✪

This ambitious wildlife rescue and rehabilitation project, scheduled to open in late 2002, is a volunteer non-profit undertaking, spearheaded by Marie Steele-Romanelli, a wildlife rehabilitator, and enthusiastically supported by the community.

Florida Birding and Wildflower Festival ✪ *850-229-5464* ✪ *www.birdfestival.org* ✪ *info@birdfestival.org*

From St. George Island to Mexico Beach, this autumn event encompasses several state parks and preserves. Some 300 enthusiasts turned up for the premiere in 2001, among them several Canadians. The 2002 program was even broader – a four-day line-up of some 70 lectures, workshops and tours with botanists and wildlife experts, boat and kayak trip, sunset hayride tours to nesting areas, an astronomical display and lighthouse tours. Registration is $25; tours and workshops cost $10 to $40.

The **Beaches of South Walton** include 18 communities, punctuating Road 30-A, which rims the seacoast between **Panama City** and **Destin**. Thanks to appealing seascapes, lovely white beaches and good fishing, this area has attracted many long-stay Canadian snowbirds. While the pace of life may be sedate, the challenges of diving and snorkeling, canoeing and hiking should appeal to younger travellers too. Since winter months are off-season here, accommodation prices drop dramatically.

You can collect splendid shells if you're prepared to venture a mile offshore where massive sandbars deliver sand dollars, cockles, sea horses and striped cowries. For divers the rewards may be even bigger – huge shells up to 10 pounds to be found along a ribbon-like reef of limestone.

An excellent website – www.30-A.com – details a year-round calendar of special events that range from Oktoberfest in **Sandestin** to wine in **Seaside** (where The Truman Story was filmed) and leads visitors on a merry virtual bike ride that stops to explore each community.

Vistas of snowy sand dunes and sea oats bending to the ocean's breezes make Panhandle beaches a joy to behold.

The Chautauqua Assembly ✪ *850-892-4300* ✪ *www.chautauqua-assembly.com* ✪ is held each February at **DeFuniak Springs**, 35 miles inland from Destin, 50 miles from Panama City. This three-day event, a winter edition of the famed Chautauqua Assembly in New York state each summer, includes classical music, theatre, writing classes, crafts, and political discussions.

The Village of Baytowne Wharf ✪ *Sandestin* ✪ *1-850-267-8135*

The company that brought Canada Tremblant Village in the Laurentians and Whistler-Blackcombe in B.C has transplanted ts village-centred resort concept to the Panhandle. The Village of Baytowne Wharf near Destin, opened in June, 2002, is at the centre of Intrawest's 2,400-acre Sandestin Golf and Beach Resort. Designed to invoke an old-world fishing village, with meandering walkways and gardens, the Village incorporates specialty merchants, boutiques, eateries and nightclubs, along with special events and happenings for all ages. Accommodations include

Panhandle waters are paradise for fisherfolk with plenty of charters and guides available.

Lodging prices drop during winter months in many parts of the Panhandle, a boon for Canadian bargain hunters.

studios, and one-, two- and three-bedroom units.

Adventures Unlimited Outdoor Center ❂ (*$-$$*) ❂ *8974 Tomahawk Landing Road, Milton* ❂ *1-800-239-6864* ❂ *www.adventuresunlimited.com*

The Panhandle's snowy beaches get all the attention and that's not fair. Head inland and you'll encounter great forests and fabulous rivers, fed by crystal springs.

Just north of Milton, on an 88-acre spread, Adventures Unlimited offers a variety of watery pursuits, with canoeing at the top of the list – not the spine-tingling white water variety, but peaceful wilderness paddling with frequent stops at sandbars along the shores. You can also kayak, tube, swim and camp.

Accommodation includes cottages (a century-old cracker house) or rustic cabins. Or stay at the 1925 School House Inn, where each of the eight rooms is named for an American author, with décor to match. A loftier option is a 'tree house', air-conditioned but without plumbing, built on 10-foot stilts to reveal the wonders of the canopy. Jack and Esther Sanborn, who created the resort in 1976, maintain a peaceable kingdom – no clocks, phones or TVs in the rooms, no pets and an alcohol-free campground. A two-night minimum applies; reservations recommended.

Destroyed by a hurricane in 1995, Pensacola's mighty fishing pier has been rebuilt -- wider, longer and made of concrete.

Pensacola

We stand corrected. We thought St. Augustine and Fernandina Beach were Florida's oldest settlements. But we were wrong. Pensacola holds that honour, thanks to settlers who struggled ashore 'way back in 1559, six years ahead of St. Augustine. What's more, the city changed hands more than a dozen times and later endured Civil War battering. Its two forts, Fort Barrancas and Fort Pickens, built after the War of 1812 and still facing off across Pensacola Bay, were held by opposing forces.

The T.T. Wentworth Jr. Florida State Museum ✪ *330 S. Jefferson St.* ✪ *840-595-5985* ✪ which reviews the area's history, architecture and archaeology, recently reopened after a $450,000 restoration project. Wentworth was another of those over-the-top collectors, amassing more than 10,000 artifacts ranging from a stuffed cat to a shrunken head to Civil War uniform buttons. The city finally recognized his efforts by dedicating the old city hall, a 1906 Mediterranean revival building, as his museum. Mon-Sat., 10-4, Adults $6, seniors $5, kids $2.50

The Civil War Soldiers Museum ✪ *108 S. Palafox St.* ✪ *850-469-1900* ✪ is another collector's treasure trove, this time Dr. Norman W. Haines, and houses one of the largest Civil War collections in the US. (Tues-Sat, 10-4:30). *The Colonial Archaeological Trail* ✪ *850-595-5985* ✪ *www.his-*

toricpensacola.org ✪ is a walking tour that visits old forts as well as the city's downtown historic district where Creole and Victorian homes from the 1780s to the 1800s have been restored

Pensacola Info: www.visitpensacola.com

and converted into shops and restaurants. *The National Museum of Naval Aviation* ✪ *1750 Radford Blvd.* ✪ *850-452-3604* ✪ *www.navel-air.org* ✪ displays over 170 vintage aircraft, spanning close to a century, from early wood-and-fabric biplanes to modern space craft. Open daily, 9-5 except Christmas, New Years and US Thanksgiving. Adm: free.

Pensacola just missed being part of Alabama by a few miles, so its ambience and etiquette reflect far more 'old South' than 'south Florida.' An annual pre-Lenten Mardi Gras replete with parades, contests and food reinforces those southern roots. (1-800-874-1234). Pensacola hosts a Great Gulf Coast Arts Festival in late fall, (www.ggaf.org) attracting hundreds of fine art and craft exhibitors, along with live entertainment. A blues fest in April, seafood in September, a Christmas festival of lights and a January 1 Polar Bear Dip that can't hold an icicle to the frigid Canuck version are among the year's highlights.

Walking tours introduce visitors to Pensacola's historic district, dating from the 1700s.

The region's 40 miles of beaches are more of the snow-white powdery sand of the Panhandle. A bit cooler than the rest of the state, the city notes an average high of 77, average low of 60, with January and February the coolest months.

When Hurricane Opal wiped out the old Pensacola fishing pier in 1995, but anglers are happy again with the new Pensacola Fishing Pier – taller, wider, longer and this time, made of concrete. It extends 1,471 feet into the Gulf of Mexico, putting anglers within reach of everything from hammerhead sharks to cobia and mackerel.

Accommodations

Florida lodgings run the gamut from ultra-luxurious to strip motels, from nation-wide chains to snug historic B&Bs, from upscale cottages to rustic wilderness cabins. Many websites and tourist brochures publish miles of lists but sorting out the wheat from the chaff is challenging. Here are some interesting alternatives.

The Superior Small Lodging Association is a group of some 500 small hotels, inns and B&Bs, most of them in Florida, where member hotels are to be found in 16 areas. Membership criteria include an annual property review covering everything from appearance to safety to bathroom and kitchen conditions to guest services. In these establishments, you pay a little more money and get a lot more real hospitality and service, as well as the unique personality of each property and its host. The program began in Fort Lauderdale in 1989 and spread rapidly throughout the state. The website (www.superiorsmalllodging.com) lets you search easily for properties in the areas you plan to visit.

Florida Bed and Breakfast Inns is another association, founded in 1995, that promotes quality and personal service. Some 140 bed & breakfast inns, country inns, small oceanfront resorts and historic hotels participate in the program that includes biannual inspections. The Association publishes a free directory that Canadians can order from 1-800-524-1880 or www.florida-inns.com.

Old St. Augustine Village is a charming oasis, surrounded by historic homes, hotels and B&Bs.

Vacation rental homes are gaining ground, especially for families. Usually close to popular attractions and equipped with every amenity from swimming pools to large-screen TVs, they're an economical and comfortable alternative to hotels or condos. Some of the companies to check out are **ResortQuest International**, which says it has 6,000 properties in Florida (www. ResortQuest.com) and **1st**

RVs enjoy outstanding campsites, including this wooded wilderness at Ginnie Springs.

Choice Vacation Properties, (www.choice1.com). Two that are located in the Kissimmee area are **Premier Vacation Homes** (www.pr-vacation.com) and **VillaDirect**, (www.villadirect.com).

Many **Florida parks**, be they national, state or regional, permit camping, some admit RVs and a few have cabins for rent. The only national forest renting cabins is **Ocala**, with two units. (www.camprrm.com). The cabins are so popular that they are allocated by lottery, conducted each May. Applications are accepted in May for the year ahead. To investigate housing and camping in state and national parks, visit www.myflorida.com and search for parks and cabins in the regions you'll be visiting.

Kampgrounds of America (KOA) has 27 locations throughout Florida. You can expect clean, well maintained and moderately priced campgrounds, with entertaining extras such as swimming pools and playgrounds. The Okeechobee KOA has a nine-hole golf course, while Fiesta Key boasts an on-site pub and a 20-unit motel. Several offer RV rentals. Many KOAs welcome tent campers and all but three rent 'kabins and kottages', for folks with neither tents nor RVs. Reservations can be made online at www.koakampgrounds.com.

El Monte RV is a California-based company, established in 1970, with offices in Orlando. The company rents RVs – everything from bus style to truck campers. Their fleet of 1,800 rental vehicles, all under two years of age, ranges from bus style to truck campers. Info: 1-800-367-3687 or www.elmonterv.com.

Border Crossings

Border crossings became more difficult after the 9/11 tragedy. In its aftermath, US Immigration moved to control the alien population within the country, by limiting visits to 30 days, instead of the previous six months. If implemented, this rule would spell an end to the Canadian snowbird phenomenon that still takes thousands of Canadian seniors to Florida each winter (and incidentally pours millions of Canadian dollars into US coffers to boot.)

Recently the INS declared that the new rules will not apply to Canadians and has promised to issue clarifying orders to immigration officers at all airports and border points indicating that Canadians are eligible for six-month stays. The problem is that border officials have broad discretionary powers and stories of their arbitrary refusals and harassment are rife.

To minimize the risk of refusal at the border, you need a Canadian pass-port (valid for several months past the date of your intended return). Information that proves your continued residency in Canada – current realty tax bills or rent receipts, phone and utility bills – are helpful. The name and number of your lawyer and federal member of parliament may be useful.

Flea markets are popular pastimes in Florida. This sprawling emporium in Oldsmar sells everything from soup to nuts, art to hubcaps, junk to junque.

Deals and Discounts

In the aftermath of 9/11, Florida became a bargain-hunter's haven. Some of those deals are still around along with the usual crop of discounts marched out in honour of Canadians. Before departure, visit the website of each area on your itinerary and look for discounts, dollars at par and other such goodies. In several cases, you can

Fanciful ceramics are a colourful commodity at Oldsmar Flea Market.

download coupons. If you're driving, stop at the official Florida visitor centres just inside the state and pick up some of the myriad discount booklets and coupons available there. (Don't bother with the so-called visitor centres before the border – unless you need a washroom.)

Some seniors' organizations offer discounts but these deals usually come with strings attached – lengthy blackout periods (major holidays) and limitations of one kind an another. Far better to phone ahead or simply march up to the reception desk and ask what discounts are on offer – Canuck, corporate, senior, veteran. You'll usually get one.

Driving

Florida's highways, deprived of Canada's winter salt and frost, are generally smooth and straight, but endowed with some truly awful drivers, who like to zoom along in high speed clumps, each vehicle about half a car-length behind the next. Posted speed limits are strictly for sissies. For information about Florida driving, roads, distances and especially current construction projects, visit www11.myflorida.com.

Speaking of speed limits, if you're stopped for speeding (as we were – once), it's wise to acknowledge it and apologize. The officers we encountered were professional and courteous, issuing a stern warning but reducing the fine.

If you drive to Florida, don't leave home without Dave Hunter's Along Interstate 75, which details the route from Detroit to the Florida border, mile by mile, complete with gas stations, restaurants, accommodation and little nuggets of local history and attractions. Updated annually, it's in bookstores or available from www.i75online.com.

Gardens

With a growing season of ten to twelve months, spectacular gardens are the norm in Florida. We couldn't visit them all but here are a few that we enjoyed.

Marie Selby Botanical gardens ❂ *811 S. Palm Ave., Sarasota* ❂ *941-366-5731* ❂ *www.selby.org* ❂ occupies only nine acres but what a show –20,000 plants, under glass and out of doors, a fabulous tropical display of orchids, bromeliads and ferns, a 6,000-sq.-ft. greenhouse that feels like a jungle rain forest, a remarkable collection of epiphytes outside in the 'live oak grove', an impressive wall of bamboo beside a waterfall garden with koi, and a banyan grove that's a popular setting for weddings and special events. Hibiscus, palms, succulents and more add to the spectacle. This place is a floral wonderland, aided and abetted by an educational mandate that includes seminars and classes, an impressive museum that doubles as art gallery and as setting for the annual December Selby by Candlelight event. There's an outstanding bookstore, and a pleasant lunch service, Michael's in the Garden. Open daily 10-5 except Christmas. Adults $10, children 6-11, $5.

Florida's public gardens, such as Marie Selby in Sarasota enjoy year-round growing season.

Harry P. Leu Gardens ❂ *1920 N. Forest Ave., Orlando* ❂ *407-246-2620* ❂ *www.leugardens.org* ❂ offers a completely different garden experience. This 50-acre site, located in a residential area of Orlando, boasts the largest

Orchids present a stunning display at Sarasota's Selby Gardens.

camellia collection in eastern North America and the largest formal rose garden in Florida. There are butterfly and herb gardens, a daylily collection and acres of tropical plants including palms, bamboos and cycads, linked by winding shady pathways. Camellias, which bloom from October to March, star in their own show, the annual Camellia Show each January. A highlight of the Gardens is House, a National Historic site, built in 1888 and restored to the style of a century ago. The last owner, Harry P. Leu, collected plants from around the world to build a garden showplace and donated the property to Orlando in 1961. Guided tours of the home are offered. Open 9-5 daily. Adults, $4, kids K-Grade 12, $1.

McKee Botanical Garden ❂ *350 South U.S. Hwy 1, Vero Beach* ❂ *561-794-0601* ❂ *www.mckeegarden.org* ❂ has re-emerged, after a 22-year hiatus, as a major attraction, just as it was half a century ago. Once known as the McKee Jungle Gardens, it served as a jungle training facility for the US Navy during World War II. Undermined by theme park madness, it was sold for development in 1976 but in 1995, local citizens created the Indian River Land Trust, and thwarted plans to build a shopping centre on the site. They raised $2.98 million to buy the site and another $6 million to renovate it. The Garden re-opened in 1991 – 18 acres of lush foliage, including 300 royal palms, flowering vines, waterways and unique historic buildings. Open Tues-Sat, 10-5, Sun 12-5. Adults, $6, children 5-12, $3.50.

Bok Tower Gardens ❂ *1151 Tower Blvd., Lake Wales,* ❂ *863-676-1408* ❂ *www.boktowergardens.org* ❂ is a National Historic Landmark dating from 1929, noted for its spectacular 'Singing Tower'. This 205-foot spire, constructed of pink and gray marble and coquina stone, houses a 60-bell carillon that peels a recital each day at 3 while clock music sounds on the half-hour from 10 am. The 157-acre woodland setting is traced with pathways, flowers and friendly animals. There's a café, gift shop and visitor centre, and complimentary wheelchairs and strollers. Open daily 8 to 6. Adults $6, children 5-12 $2, under 5 free. Saturday 8-9 free.

What could be sweeter than a long , lazy tubing expedition down a broad gentle river in Northwest Florida.

Sports

You'll be hard pressed to name a sport that isn't available in Florida. Of course the sea and rivers provide fabulous boating, kayaking, canoeing, fishing, snorkeling and diving. Further inland, there's hiking, horseback riding and myriad wilderness adventures.

Two spectator sports you're unlikely to see in Canada are jai alai and greyhound racing, a practice that is widely opposed as inhumane.

Jai alai (pronounced hi li) is a fast and rowdy sport, an import from Europe's Basque Country, via Cuba, about a century ago. It's played on a three-walled court, with a hard ball somewhat smaller than a baseball, propelled at speeds up to 150 mph by a curved basket, comparable to a lacrosse stick. A typical game comprises 14 rounds of about 15 minutes each. You'll find jai alai frontons (courts) in Ocala, Orlando, Dania and Miami. Wagering is brisk.

For many visitors, **golf** is the number one sports activity in Florida and outstanding golf courses, blessed with year-round weather, are far too numerous to mention. Each community and county touts its own area courses and numerous websites offer information on courses, schools, tee-times and nearby accommodations. Try www.playfloridagolf.com and www.floridagolfguide.com.

Florida is spring training base for baseball teams. Practice sessions are usually free while **'grapefruit league'** games, usually throughout the month of March, cost under US$15. **The Blue Jays** practice at Dunedin on the west coast, the **Montreal Expos** at Jupiter (above Fort Lauderdale) on the east coast. You can order tickets after Jan 2 at 1-800-707-8269.

Theme Parks

Florida's myriad theme parks scarcely fall into the 'undiscovered, unsung, unspoiled' classification that rules this book. Still, you may decide to combine a theme park with an unknown aspect of Florida.

Best news at **Disney** is the arrival of Canada's **Cirque du Soleil**, presenting two 90-minute shows, Thursday to Monday at 6 and 9 p.m. Tickets: Adults $67, Kids 3-9 $39. (407-939-7719.) **The Animal Kingdom** is a pleasant and somewhat educational look at exotic animals. **DisneyQuest** is a high-tech entertainment centre packed with games and rides, including one that lets you design your own rollercoaster and then ride a simulated version of it.

At nearby **Universal Studios**, the space is smaller but the atmosphere more upbeat, especially at Islands of Adventure where attractions include Spiderman, the Hulk, Men in Black Alien Attack and Back to the Future.

Busch Gardens in Tampa Bay is a taste of Africa – several tastes, really – with up-close views of hundreds of African animals in natural environments. An innovation that we hope will continue is the 'Rain Guarantee' program allowing a free return visit within seven days if rain ruins your day at the Park.

Cypress Gardens near Winter Haven, is the grand-daddy of Florida theme parks established 1935. It encompasses vast outdoor floral displays, ice shows, a butterfly house and a new water park. Its seasonal shows are impressive, especially the holiday spectacle, late November to early January, which showcases more than 40,000 red, pink and white poinsettias within a fantasy setting of twinkling lights, waterfalls, streams and a two-level garden railway plus a 20-foot poinsettia tree.

Lovely vistas of flowers and a gazebo have made Cypress Gardens a favourite for almost 70 years.

Weddings

Getting married in Florida is easy. There's no waiting period for non-residents – the couple simply turns up at a courthouse with passports or driver's licenses and buys a marriage license for $88.50 (cash or credit card.) You need proof of divorce if previously married, a death certificate if previous spouse died.

And where to tie the knot? There must be at least a million romantic and picturesque locales from which to choose – beaches, gardens, parks, historic buildings. The choice narrows somewhat for couples who want location, reception and even their honeymoon in a single place. Many resorts, hotels and B&Bs offer just such a facility. Larger hotels have resident wedding coordinators attending to every detail. Less formal but infinitely charming are B&Bs such as the Rosslor Manor in Ocala (page 31) and the Emerald Hill B&B near Mount Dora (page 72), whose hosts are qualified to perform wedding ceremonies.

One-stop wedding service is available at **Steinhatchee Landing Resort** in north-central Florida thanks to a new wedding chapel along with six charming honeymoon cottages (with two more to come). With a total of 30 houses, plus the 17-room **Steinhatchee River Inn** just down the road, and a well appointed conference centre which can handle up to 100 guests for the reception, an entire wedding party including the guests can take over the Resort and party on.

The new wedding chapel, set within a dramatic grove of trees, is a Gothic inspired design, built of stone with 16-foot ceilings, fine stained glass windows and seating for 80 people. The Resort's wedding package includes food services, wedding planning, officiating clergy or notary, flowers and photos. (See also page 146).

Two of our favourite Florida boats cater for weddings. **Captain Conrad's 'Black Tie'**(see page 117) in Fort Myers, a lovingly restored 1936 wooden vessel is a romantic spot both for a honeymoon and for the ceremony too. Black Tie's wedding planner, Glory Williams, will plan and even perform the wedding.

In Sanford, the **Rivership Romance**, (see page 65), a triple-decked river cruiser, offers several settings for the ceremony plus onboard banquet and entertainment facilities for up to 400 guests.

St. Augustine's historic buildings and lush gardens make for perfect weddings.

A flower decked carriage drawn by two fine grays adds a special touch to a wedding in Ocala.

St. Francis Inn (1-800-824-6062) plays host to many weddings, some-times spilling over to its sister inn, the **Casa de Solana** and the historic **Llambas House** nearby. The inn's walled courtyard is ideal for intimate garden weddings while larger groups may adjourn to neighbouring his-toric buildings.

Amore Wedding Chapel in the 1903 Xavier Lopez house (904-826-0715) seats up to 50 people. A winding staircase makes a picturesque entrance for the bride and after the ceremony, the couple join hands to 'ring the wedding bell' on the front verandah. A DJ, changing room and reception space for 40 guests indoors or 125 outdoors are available.

In **Ocala**, Florida's horse capital, Mary Garland plans unique weddings, complete with a flower-decked white carriage drawn by two fine horses to transport the wedding couple. (See page 181).

Another popular wedding venue is the gazebo chapel at **Cypress Gardens** in Winter Haven, (Hwy. 27, south of I-4), the setting for more than 500 weddings each year. The gazebo is perched on a hilltop, and the gardens are a riot of colour with some 8,000 plants and flowers bor-dering the walkways. Wedding staff can arrange all the details, from limos to catering, photography and officiating clergy. Info: www.cypress-gardens.com or 1-800-282-2123.

Insurance

It's madness to head into the US – and especially Florida -- without travel health insurance. Florida medical practitioners and hospitals are expensive – very, very expensive. And not all of them are scrupulous about their billing practices.

Canada's provincial plans will pay for out-of-country medical expenses exactly what they pay for in-country – and that's a tiny fraction of Florida prices. So a fall or a car accident can cost you a bundle. And major illness, surgery or treatment could cost you your life savings.

Up-close encounters with exotic wildlife are a special treat in Florida.

Out-of-country insurance falls into various categories – single trip, annual plan and long-stay. We buy the Canadian Automobile Association annual plan, which allows unlimited trips of 30 days or less (top-ups are available). Fortunately we've never faced a crisis, but other users tell us that CAA acts quickly and fairly to settle claims. Insurance is also available from travel agents, and from various independent companies such as Voyageur and TravMark, and some credit cards include insurance (but beware – you may only be covered if you purchase your trip with your credit card).

If you're planning a long-stay of several months, the picture changes and so do the prices. The price jumps with each decade of your age and with medical conditions or changes in medication (which can mean discontinued, increased or changed to a different dosage.) Some companies refuse to insure persons past the age of 80 or those with pre-existing conditions, no matter how stable.

Visit our website

Our lively new website is working to provide you with updates on properties and attractions, news of new and interesting developments in 'undiscovered, unsung, unspoiled Florida'. Please pay a visit to **www.florida-eh.com** and leave us a message. Your suggestions, comments and informed tips will be invaluable in making the website – and the next edition of Florida, Eh?, the book – even more informative.

Every policy is couched in double-speak that, like it or not, you absolutely must read and understand. Some are so ambiguous as to rank as gobbledy-gook and that's intentional. When it comes time to settle a claim, the insurance company has the final world on interpreting its policy.

Insurance is a lucrative business and various seniors' organizations such as Canadian Snowbirds Association and Canadian Association of Retired Persons offer policies, some claiming to be in 'plain English' that even we can understand.

Until a decade or so ago, provincial government health plans paid the full shot for out-of-country health care. Billions of Canadian dollars poured into US medical coffers before the governments pulled the plug and mainstream insurance companies, who know a thing or two about obfuscation and deception, moved to fill the void. They were joined by a sleazy pack of pirates, flogging bargain-priced policies that usually failed to deliver when customers filed claims.

So the message is: Caveat Emptor – buyer beware. Given the multi-million dollar profits that insurance companies report each quarter, you can reasonably conclude that they are suffering somewhat less than the hapless travelers whose premiums line their spacious pockets.

Snow-white beaches of Sanibel Island are popular with sunbathers and shell pickers.

Safety and Security

Tourists are sitting ducks for all manner of criminals. Though some Florida cities, notably Miami, have adopted dramatic measures to reduce crime, each one of us must take steps to protect ourselves, especially in congested areas. Mostly it's common sense, which sometimes takes a holiday when we do.

Exquisite butterfly, thorny thistle – a colourful wilderness combo.

Here are some safety tips to consider:

Never look lost. If you need to check a map or ask directions, do so in a public place. Ask for directions before sallying forth. Keep doors and windows locked. Lock luggage or packages in the trunk and out of sight.

Don't stop if you're bumped or signaled. Drive on and dial 911 if you have a cell phone. Always check your car's interior before getting in.

Choose a handbag with a short strap so it can tuck under your arm. Carry your wallet in an inside jacket pocket – never in your hip pocket. Keep wads of bills under wraps – with automatic banking machines in widespread use, it's easy to replenish your cash supply.

Pickpockets and airport thieves often use distraction techniques – one will drop some coins or ask for directions while an accomplice makes off with your bags or wallet. Be alert to their ploys.

In your hotel, be wary of sliding doors and windows. Be sure they're locked. Do not admit anyone to your room, not

Phone numbers

Although many Florida inns advertise toll-free numbers, very few extend that courtesy to Canadians. As well, the state's telephone area codes are changing. We've done our best to provide current numbers, but these two factors may result in calls that can't be completed. Do remind innkeepers that Canadians comprise a huge market in Florida and the courtesy of a toll-free number is simply good business.

even a hotel employee without first verifying with the front desk that they are on legitimate business. Keep valuables in the safe and don't leave jewelry or cash lying about.

Weather

It's 'the sunshine state', right? So sunshine is the order of most days, (don't forget your sun block), sometimes interrupted by a brief, warm tropical rain in the afternoon. Panhandle temperatures are moderate year-round while the mercury rises as you proceed south. Summer and fall are the season for hurricanes and tropical storms, which may attack not only the east coast but the Gulf as well. The National Weather Service provides authoritative information on storms, and the weather in general, at www.nws.noaa.gov. Also keeping track of hurricanes is www.spacebag.com/hurricane.htm.

Wilderness and Parks

National parks, state parks, county parks and regional sanctuaries and preserves combine to provide Florida with an unbelievable wealth of wilderness opportunities. There are 1.25 million acres of federal public lands, encompassing both parks and forests; 157 state parks and numerous valuable but largely unsung regional parks and preserves. Check websites for the areas on your itinerary or visit www.myflorida.com or www.dep.state.fl.us/parks. For federal parks see http://www.nps.gov/; for national forests, visit www.southernregion.fs.fed.us/florida.

Florida's eastern shoreline is a year-round haven for shore birds and a migratory path for many species.

Florida by word of mouse
by Anne Dimon

Most Florida-bound travellers start their research at the Visit Florida website (www.flausa.com) which in turn links to the various Convention and Visitor Bureaus throughout the state. The Flausa site provides an overview of the state, plus neat tools like an interactive map that lets you zoom in on main cities in various regions. But it does have limitations – both Flausa and local CVBs are partner organizations. Only partners enjoy website listings and links. So unusual attractions or properties, however worthy, appear only if they've purchased memberships.

To jump directly to the official travel sites of individual regions, check out www.officialtravelinfo.com. Type Florida into the search bar and within seconds you pull up info on over three dozen tourist areas.

One of the best and most comprehensive sites, especially for special interest travel,is www.stateofflorida.com. The URL rings of government bureaucracy, but it's actually operated by Livingston North Communications based in Orlando and it dishes up pretty much everything a visitor might need to know about the Sunshine State. For special interest travel (stuff like birding, fishing, hiking or RV campsites), open the Tourism and Travel section to pull up an alphabetized list of categories with links. Other departments worth a browse are Florida Facts, Kid Stuff and City & Counties. The latter offers maps and directions.

Sanibel is small in size but richly endowed with family-friendly parks and wildlife sanctuaries.

To get reviews of 35 top tourist attractions plus links to downloadable discount coupons on a good number of them go to www.touristflorida.com. For more on attractions, discounts and special promotions try www.floridaattractions.com where you can search by attraction,

Our lively new website is working to provide you with updates on properties and attractions, news of new and interesting developments in 'undiscovered, unsung, unspoiled Florida'.

Please pay a visit to **www.florida-eh.com** and leave us a message. Your suggestions, comments and informed tips will be invaluable in making the website – and the next edition of Florida, Eh?, the book – even more informative.

category (things like animal parks or historical) or region.

What's happening throughout the state during your visit? Florida Festival and Events Association posts listings at www.ffea.org. You can search by type of event, month and city. Listings then give you phone numbers, e-mails and event web sites.

Billed as "an insider's guide to unique destinations," www.floridasecrets.com gives you ideas for adventures and excursions from sailing charters off Amelia Island to diving for shark teeth in Venice. A section on bed and breakfast establishments pulls up descriptions, photos and contact information.

Florida Outdoors, at www.florida-outdoors.com points you toward such activities as fishing, hunting, camping, canoeing and wildlife watching. The Feature Articles section delivers about a dozen professionally-written stories about activities like alligator hunting, eco-touring, fly fishing and birding.

Are you a Canadian Snowbird thinking of your winter getaway? Canadian lawyer and author Andrew Cumming posts the online adaptation of his book Florida Bound: *The Essential Guide for Canadian Snowbirds* at www.floridabound.com. It offers, along with other travel-related stuff, basic and clear explanations on the legal rigmarole of extended stays.

Other sites to consider when planning a Florida holiday include www.fl-travel.com/theme-parks.html for theme and water parks, www.floridagolfguide.com for an online catalogue of over 1,200 Florida golf courses, and www.flamuseums.org for a database of over 340 museums.

Anne Dimon

Anne Dimon is the Internet travel columnist for the Toronto Star, Halifax Herald, Calgary Herald and Tripeze.com.

Index

UNDISCOVERED, UNSPOILED, UNSUNG...

$$$$$

**Unless otherwise specified,
all prices are in US dollars.**

Acknowledgements

Our Sincere Thanks ...

To all the generous Florida folk, whether private people, Convention and Visitor Bureaux or businesses, who shared their time, information and trade secrets to steer us toward 'the undiscovered, unsung, unspoiled' treasures that are featured in Florida, Eh?

On the homefront, maintained and patrolled by P'tit Guy et Grand Guy, we especially thank our intrepid cat/house sitters – Monika Brown and the Sussman family (Joel, Margaret, Jenny and Mark), who kept the guys fed, groomed and royally entertained during the long weeks of our research trips. Thanks are also due to the world's best neighbours, Clifford and Jean White, who watched over our home during our absence.

Our family and friends have been a constant source of inspiration and comfort. We're especially grateful to Paul Chvostek of IT Canada whose programming skills, Internet savvy and business acumen have helped us immeasurably as we navigate the shoals of e-business and develop our website.

Photographs ...

Most of the photographs in this book are by co-author Milan Chvostek.

We acknowledge with thanks the photos loaned by Visit Florida, including the front cover shells, and those on pages 168, 169 and 171. Our thanks also to the Morse Museum (pages 41, 42), Courtyard at Lake Lucerne (page 45), Daytona Beach CVB (pages 55, 56, 57), Florida Keys and Key West Tourism Development Council (page 102), Pensacola CVB (pages 167, 170), Cypress Gardens (page 179).

Special thanks to photographers Debbie Hooper (page 165) and Sandra Peic (pages 86, 87, 90, 91, 92).

Visit our website

Our lively new website is working to provide you with updates on properties and attractions, news of new and interesting developments in 'undiscovered, unsung, unspoiled Florida'. Please pay a visit to **www.florida-eh.com** and leave us a message. Your suggestions, comments and tips will be invaluable in making the website – and the next edition of Florida, Eh?, the book – even more informative.